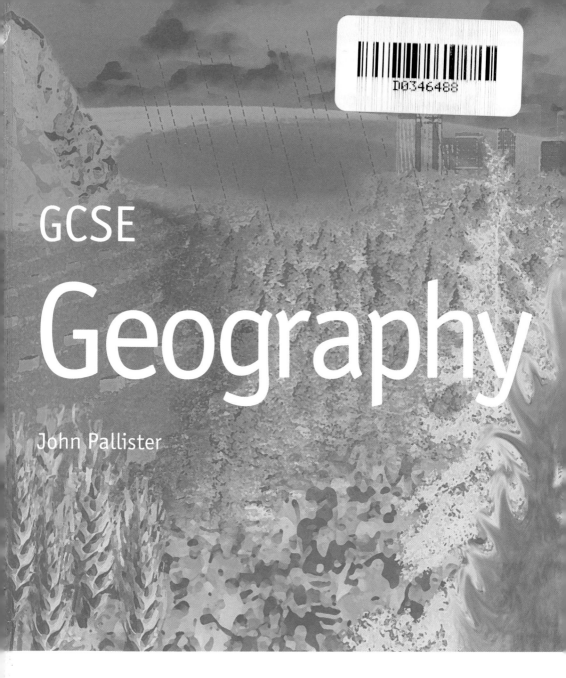

GCSE
Geography

John Pallister

ESSENTIAL WORD
DICTIONARY

Philip Allan Updates
Market Place
Deddington
Oxfordshire
OX15 0SE

Orders
Bookpoint Ltd, 130 Milton Park, Abingdon, Oxfordshire, OX14 4SB
tel: 01235 827720
fax: 01235 400454
e-mail: uk.orders@bookpoint.co.uk
Lines are open 9.00 a.m.–5.00 p.m., Monday to Saturday, with a 24-hour
message answering service. You can also order through the Philip Allan
Updates website: www.philipallan.co.uk

© Philip Allan Updates 2001

ISBN-13 978-0-86003-390-5
ISBN-10 0-86003-390-2

Printed in Spain

Philip Allan Updates' policy is to use papers that are natural, renewable
and recyclable products and made from wood grown in sustainable forests.
The logging and manufacturing processes are expected to conform to the
environmental regulations of the country of origin.

P00835

Introduction

This dictionary contains around 400 of the geographical terms which are used most often in GCSE geography. A one-sentence definition is given first for each term. This is followed by an extended definition, and examples when they are needed.

The amount of detail that is given reflects the importance of the term. For example, some entries are short and self-contained. Look at **capital city**. The one-sentence definition is supported by only one sentence of further detail. It is a basic geographical term, but it is never going to form the basis for a long GCSE answer. Now look at **birth rate**. This entry is much longer because it is an important term, studied in the population section of every GCSE specification. It includes elaboration of, and explanation for, the different birth rates in MEDCs and LEDCs.

In many of the entries, one or more words are printed in *italics*. These are cross-references to words which are defined elsewhere in the dictionary. Look at **demographic transition model**. This term cannot be understood without knowledge of other key terms, like *birth rate*, *death rate* and *natural increase*.

Another feature of this dictionary is the exam watch boxes. These contain advice which is intended to help you in your examinations. Many GCSE geography questions ask you to give two sides. You might be asked to give views for and against a particular issue, or to show knowledge of the short-term and long-term effects of an event. Some of the exam watch boxes indicate how a term can be viewed from two sides. For example:

- arguments for and against (see **dam**)
- causes and effects (see **acid rain**)
- costs and benefits (see **ageing population**)
- natural and human causes (see **flood**)
- views in favour and against (see **nuclear power**)

Case studies are used in every geography course. Short examples are given in some of the exam watch boxes, such as the entries for **inner city** and **market gardening**. These are included for two main reasons. One is to show you that you don't need a great mass of information for most case studies. Often a few key facts, used in the right place, are all that is needed for a successful examination answer. The second is to guide you into arranging case study information under headings. Never write down all the information you can find, because (a) you won't be able to learn it all, and (b) if you do, you won't have time in the examination to use it.

Finally, there is more to answering examination questions than merely having the knowledge. You have to know how best to use this information by obeying the command words. In all questions, you should try to identify the command word (or words). Two command words commonly used in GCSE geography questions are 'describe' and 'explain', but they require totally different types of answer.

Take a look at the exam watch box under the entry for **corrie**. It gives examples of a 'describe' question and an 'explain' question, and provides answers for both. It doesn't matter if you haven't studied this landform. Most of the answer to the 'describe' question can be taken from the sketch. However, to give a full answer, geographical knowledge of other terms is needed. In this example they are 'arête', 'tarn lake' and 'scree'. The answer given to the 'explain' question is totally different. None of it can be taken from the sketch. Knowledge and understanding of glacial and weathering processes are needed before the question can be attempted.

There is an element of luck with questions in all examinations, but you can increase the chances of having good luck in your GCSE geography exams by knowing and understanding the key terms in this dictionary.

abrasion (also called 'corrasion'): wearing away of the Earth's surface by rocks transported by rivers, waves or glaciers.

Abrasion is a process of *erosion*.

River abrasion — rivers transport rocks and boulders. These are knocked against the bottom and sides of the river channel, eroding both the channel and the transported material itself. Most erosion occurs in times of *flood*.

Coastal abrasion — waves erode the coastline by flinging pebbles against *cliff* faces. This happens most during storms, when high and powerful waves, known as *destructive waves*, batter the coast.

Glacial abrasion — rocks with sharp edges are carried in the bottom of a moving *glacier*. These rocks are driven into the ground by the great weight of the ice and act like giant files, scratching and eroding the ground surface.

acid lava: thick and sticky *lava* thrown out by some *volcanoes*, mainly along *destructive plate boundaries*.

Acid lava has a high silica content. It flows slowly and thickly, often only over short distances. Acid lava builds up around the *crater* to form an *acid lava volcano*.

acid lava volcano: dome-shaped *volcano*, with steep sides and a narrow base.

Explosive eruptions are common.

acid rain: rainwater made more acid by air pollution.

Pollutants present in the atmosphere, notably sulphur dioxide and oxides of nitrogen, are dissolved in rain as it falls. This increases the acidity of the rain by the time it reaches the ground.

Causes of acid rain
- large amounts of sulphur dioxide and oxides of nitrogen emitted from coal and oil-fired power stations
- sulphur dioxide and oxides of nitrogen emitted by factories and vehicle exhausts

Effects of acid rain
- trees die
- soils become too acid for crops to grow well and yields are reduced
- fish die because lakes become too acid for plant and other animal life to thrive
- stone buildings and statues, especially those made of limestone, are damaged and dissolved away

Levels of acid rain can be reduced by:
- removing sulphur dioxide before it is emitted from power stations
- using different fossil fuels which release fewer pollutants (e.g. *natural gas*) or energy from *renewable resources* (e.g. *hydroelectric power* and *wind power*)
- making catalytic converters compulsory on cars

ageing population: increasing percentage of old people (aged 65 and over) in a country.

Populations are ageing fastest in *MEDCs*, where people are living longer as a result of improvements in medical knowledge and treatment. In the UK, the percentage of young people is going down because the *birth rate* is low. By about 2015, it is estimated that for the first time the number of people aged 65 and over will be greater than the number of people under 16.

Costs of an ageing population to a country
- governments must pay out more on pensions
- more money needs to be spent on health and care services for the elderly
- these costs have to be funded by increased taxes

Benefits of an ageing population to a country
- holiday companies, like Saga, make money by taking old people on holidays outside the peak school holiday periods
- leisure and sporting clubs, such as bingo, golf and bowls, have customers all week and not just at weekends
- some companies specialise in making products for old people, such as chair lifts and wheelchairs

exam watch

agribusiness: type of farming that is run as big business.

High *inputs* of capital are invested in machinery, seeds, buildings, *fertilisers* and pesticides. *Outputs* are also high to cover costs and make profits. This is an example of *intensive farming*. East Anglia in the UK has many agribusinesses which obtain high yields of barley, wheat, sugar beet, vegetables and oil seed rape. The opposite of agribusiness occurs where farming is as much a way of life as a business, and the farm only makes a little money, such as a hill sheep farmer in the Lake District.

■ *e.g.* Companies such as Findus and Bird's Eye own and run farms, as does the Co-op.

aid: money or help given to a country in need.
■ Aid may include food, medical supplies, goods, equipment and people with special skills. There are different types of aid:
● **Bilateral aid** — aid from one government to another. Usually, the *MEDC* will provide goods, equipment and technology to the *LEDC*, often for large-scale projects such as dams, roads and power stations. The MEDC decides which projects it will support. This is also called 'tied aid', because the LEDC is not free to do what it wants with the aid being given.
● **Multilateral aid** — aid from international organisations, such as the United Nations. Governments from MEDCs provide the funds, but through its organisations the UN decides how the money is spent, e.g. UNICEF helps children and UNESCO funds education.
● **Voluntary aid** — aid from charities, such as Oxfam and Christian Aid. These fund small-scale local projects, e.g. supplying clean water and building schools and clinics in villages in LEDCs. Some regard this as the best type of aid because it is given with no strings attached.

Short-term aid
Emergency or disaster aid given after an area has been affected by a *natural hazard*, such as an *earthquake* or *drought*. The urgent need is for food, medical help and shelter.

Long-term aid
Development aid, such as digging wells, training farmers and engineers, and building new roads.

alluvium: sand and silt deposited by a river.
■ Every time a river *floods* it leaves a layer of fine-grained sediment on its *floodplain* or in its *delta*. This accumulates into thick layers over the years. Alluvium makes some of the world's most fertile soils.

alternative energy: electricity generated from *renewable resources*.
■ Forms of alternative energy include *hydroelectric, wind, solar, geothermal* and *tidal power*. They use resources provided by nature, such as weather and water, which means that they will never run out. The term 'alternative' is used because these sources of energy can be used to substitute *fossil fuels*, such as coal and oil. Alternative energy sources are cleaner and more environmentally friendly than fossil fuels.

anticyclone: area of *high pressure*.
■ Sinking air leads to greater weight and therefore higher than average pressure on the Earth's surface. In the northern hemisphere, the air which has descended

blows outwards from the centre in a clockwise direction. When an anticyclone dominates the UK's weather, it is usually dry and calm. In summer, the weather can be sunny and hot, leading to heat waves. In winter, the weather can be clear and cold, leading to frost and fog at night. The opposite of an anticyclone is a *depression*.

appropriate technology (also called 'intermediate technology'): level of technology suitable for local people to use.

■ High technology is unsuited to many people in *LEDCs*. For example, a water pump running on electricity can provide much more water than a pump operated by people or animals. But how many people in villages in LEDCs can afford the electricity? What happens when there are power cuts? Who can do the repairs? A smaller but more reliable supply of water from a hand-operated pump may be better (i.e. more appropriate) in this situation.

aquifer: underground store of water in *permeable rock*.

arable farming: type of agriculture based on growing crops, such as wheat and potatoes.

■ Some arable farmers grow crops for sale. This is an example of *commercial farming*. In the UK there are many commercial arable farms in East Anglia and the Vale of York. In *LEDCs* commercial farmers grow crops such as coffee and bananas (see *plantation*). Some arable farmers, mainly in LEDCs, grow crops to feed themselves and their families. This is *subsistence farming*. Rice growing in the Ganges valley in India is an example. The opposite of arable farming is *pastoral farming*.

arch: rocky opening through a *headland*, formed by waves.

■ An arch is a landform of coastal *erosion*. It forms where two caves are eroded backwards until daylight shows through the headland. Arches commonly occur where rocks containing many *joints* outcrop as headlands. These joints can be widened by waves.

■ *e.g.* Durdle Door in Dorset.

arête: two-sided, knife-edged mountain peak.

■ An arête is a steep-sided and narrow rock ridge which forms between the backwalls of two *corries*. It is formed by two different processes:

● *freeze–thaw* on the headwall — pieces of rock are broken off by frost shattering
● glacial *erosion* concentrated at the base of the backwall of the corrie
  When this happens on two sides, the ridge of rock becomes narrower and narrower.

■ *e.g.* Striding Edge on Helvellyn mountain in the Lake District.

arid: describes a place which receives little rain.

■ Many arid areas are *deserts*, where total precipitation is less than 250 mm per year. The largest area of desert is the Sahara in Africa. Great heat leads to rapid *evaporation* and shortage of surface water. Some areas are arid for only part of the year. India, for example, has a wet *monsoon* season and a dry season.

aspect: direction in which a slope, building or settlement faces.

■ In the northern hemisphere, south-facing slopes receive more sun and are warmer than north-facing slopes. The steeper the slope and the deeper the valley, the greater is the temperature difference between south-facing and north-facing slopes. In upland areas, this leads to important differences in *land use* between the two sides of a valley. South-facing slopes are more likely to be settled and farmed.

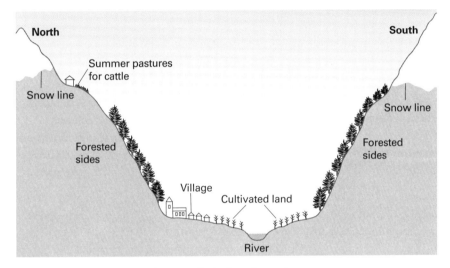

The cross-section shows that south-facing slopes have:
- a higher snow line
- summer pastures on a high level bench
- a smaller area of forest
- settlements on the valley floor

attrition: reduction in size of rocks, stones and particles while being transported.

■ Attrition is a process of *erosion*. Rocks, stones and particles are broken down into smaller pieces by colliding with one another or with the rocky beds over which they are passing. Attrition is the main reason why pebbles on beaches and in rivers are usually smooth and rounded. Pebbles are eventually reduced to sand-sized grains, which rivers and waves can transport more easily.

backwash: return flow of water out to sea after a wave breaks.

■ Backwash carries sand and shingle back into the sea. *Destructive waves* have a strong backwash which removes eroded materials, such as rocks and stones, from the bottom of *cliffs*.

bar: ridge of sand and shingle across the entrance to a *bay* or river *mouth*.

■ A bar is a landform of coastal *deposition*. Some bars grow all the way across an entrance so that a stretch of water is cut off and dammed. A lagoon, such as the pool behind Looe Bar in Cornwall, is formed.

barrage: *dam* built across an *estuary*.

■ Barrages are built for different reasons:

- as a flood defence against rising sea levels, e.g. the Netherlands
- to create *tidal power*, e.g. the Rance estuary in Brittany
- to renovate an area, e.g. Cardiff Bay (the barrage was used to create a lake around which old dockland areas were improved and modernised)

basic lava: thin and runny *lava* thrown out by some *volcanoes*, mainly along *constructive plate boundaries*.

■ Basic lava has a low silica content. It may flow for many kilometres before cooling. When the lava cools, it forms basalt rocks. The volcanic cone which forms has a wide base and gentle slopes, and is known as a *shield volcano*.

bay: large indentation of a coastline, usually between two rocky *headlands*.

■ A bay is a landform of coastal *erosion*. It often has a semi-circular shape. Bays form where soft (less resistant) rocks outcrop between hard (more resistant) rocks along the coast. The soft rocks are more easily and more quickly eroded by waves to create a bay. A beach often forms in the head of a bay.

■ *e.g.* Many seaside resorts in the UK are located at bays. For example, Scarborough has a North Bay and a South Bay with the Castle Headland in between.

beach: area of deposited materials between the high and low water marks, sloping down towards the sea.

b

■ A beach is a landform of coastal *deposition*. Sand, shingle and pebbles are the most common beach deposits. A beach is wide when the tide is out, but narrow at high tide. Shingle beaches are steeper than sandy beaches. Formation of beaches is favoured by:
● a sheltered location, such as in a *bay* or after a bend in the coastline
● *longshore drift* carrying a lot of sediment from further along the coast
● *constructive waves* that allow beach deposits to accumulate over time

bedding plane: horizontal line of weakness between layers of *sedimentary rock*.

biodiversity: level of plant and animal variety in an *ecosystem*.
■ The highest levels of biodiversity are found in *tropical rainforests*. This is because the climate is hot and wet all year round, giving ideal growing conditions for many varieties of plants.

biological weathering: breakdown of rock by plants and animals.
■ Tree roots follow *joints* in limestone rocks. They widen the joints and weaken the rock, so that it eventually shatters. As vegetation decomposes, organic acids are produced which speed up the *chemical weathering* of the rocks below.

birth rate: number of live births per 1,000 people per year.
■ The average birth rate is 13 per 1,000 in *MEDCs* and 27 per 1,000 in *LEDCs*. In general, a low birth rate shows that a country is more economically developed. Birth rates in all European Union countries are below 15 per 1,000. This is because:
● family planning is widely available
● women are well educated and wish to pursue their own careers
● one or two children is accepted as the normal family size
● children are expensive and do not contribute to family income until they are adults
A high birth rate shows that a country is less economically developed. Many countries in Africa and the Middle East have birth rates of over 40 per 1,000. This is because:
● family planning is not widely available, especially in rural areas
● many women receive little education and marry young
● families of five or more children are considered to be quite normal
● children are seen as useful for supplementing the family income and for looking after parents in their old age
● some governments and religions do not approve of birth control

boulder clay: glacial deposit, usually a mixture of clay and boulders of many different sizes.
■ Boulder clay is the name for all materials deposited by a *glacier*. These materials are unsorted and usually have sharp edges. Many of the lowland areas of the British Isles are covered by boulder clay dating from the last *ice age*. Deposits

can be found anywhere north of a line between London and Bristol. The land surface is often undulating (sloping gently up and down).

bridging point: crossing point over a river.

■ A bridging point is a favourable *situation* for a settlement, especially if there are long distances between river crossing points. The lowest bridging point (the last bridge over a river before it reaches the sea) is the most important. A settlement almost always grows up as a route centre at this place, because it is where land and sea routes meet. London and Newcastle-upon-Tyne are lowest bridging point settlements.

brown earth: main type of soil found in the British Isles.

■ Brown earth forms under deciduous woodland. It is a uniform brown colour. Many minerals can be found in the top half of the soil, which is why brown earth is more fertile than *podsol*.

brownfield site: area of previously built-up land that is available to be built on again.

■ Most brownfield sites are in inner urban areas, especially *inner city* and dockland locations. In many port cities in the UK, these sites have been used for *urban redevelopment* schemes. Examples are London Docklands, Albert Dock in Liverpool, Salford Quays in Greater Manchester and Quayside in Newcastle-upon-Tyne. It is government policy to build on brownfield sites rather than *greenfield sites*.

Burgess model: model which divides urban areas into *land use* zones.

■ Five major land use zones are arranged in a circular pattern. In the centre is the *central business district*. Surrounding it are areas of manufacturing and housing. The housing (residential) areas increase in status and value with increasing distance from the centre.

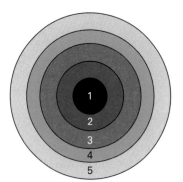

1 Central business district (CBD)
2 Inner city
3 Older residential suburbs
4 Newer residential suburbs
5 Rural–urban fringe

business park: area laid out for offices, usually located *out-of-town*.

■ A business park is a modern type of *industrial estate* which includes offices, warehouses for distribution and small factories. Call centres are an example of the type of company that uses business parks. The most common location for a business park is on a *greenfield site*. The advantages are:

- proximity to major lines of transport, especially motorways
- pleasant location surrounded by countryside
- space for car parking and landscaped areas

Business parks built specifically for *high-tech industries* are known as *science parks*.

CAP: see *Common Agricultural Policy.*

capital: money invested into industries and businesses.
▣ Capital is an *input*. Money is needed for both starting up a business and expanding it. The money pays for other inputs, such as *raw materials, energy* and *labour*. It also finances equipment and machinery, such as computers and robots. Some industries are capital-intensive (they use a lot of capital). *Heavy industries* are capital-intensive because they have bulky raw materials and use massive amounts of machinery. *High-tech industries* also need a lot of capital to fund research and development of new ideas and products.

capital city: city where the government of a country is located.
▣ A capital city is the political centre of a country, where important decisions which affect the entire population are taken.

Carboniferous limestone: type of *sedimentary rock.*
▣ Carboniferous limestone weathers to form distinctive surface and underground features known as *karst*. Limestone *solution* is responsible for the formation of many of these features. In the UK, Carboniferous limestone outcrops in parts of the Yorkshire and Derbyshire Dales.

cash crop: crop grown for sale instead of for the farmer's own use.
▣ Cultivation of a cash crop is an example of *commercial farming*. The opposite is *subsistence farming.*

cave: either a landform of coastal *erosion* or an underground feature of *karst* scenery.
▣ On the coast, a cave is an area which has been hollowed by waves at the bottom of a cliff. Waves attack and widen lines of weakness, by processes such as *abrasion* and *hydraulic action*. In areas of *Carboniferous limestone*, caves form where underground streams flow along lines of weakness, such as *bedding planes*. The bedding planes are widened into caves by limestone *solution* and the force of flowing water.

cavern: large underground chamber, larger than a *cave*, in areas of *Carboniferous limestone*.

▥ A cavern is a feature of *karst*.

▥ *e.g.* The largest cavern in the UK is below Gaping Gill near Ingleton, which is more than 30 m high and 150 m long.

CBD: see *central business district*.

central business district (CBD): urban zone located in a city (or town) centre, dominated by shops and offices.

▥ The central business district is located in the centre of an urban area, around the historical *core*. The main difference between a CBD and other urban zones is that few people live there. From a distance, a CBD can often be recognised by the concentration of skyscrapers and other tall buildings. Compared with other urban zones, a CBD:

- has the largest offices and shops, including department stores
- has the widest variety of goods for sale
- has high land values, rents and rates, so that many buildings are tall and built close together
- is the main place of work by day, leading to traffic congestion
- is at the most accessible location, where main roads (and railways) meet

exam watch

To identify the location of a town's CBD on an OS map, two or more of the following pieces of evidence are needed:
- meeting of A-roads (sometimes leading into an inner ring road)
- the main railway station (usually on its edge)
- presence of historical buildings, such as a cathedral or castle
- heavily built-up area with few open spaces

chalk: type of *sedimentary rock*.

▥ Water can pass underground through chalk. This means that there is little drainage over the surface. It resists erosion well and forms *escarpments* inland and *cliffs* along coasts. Chalk outcrops in many parts of southern England. For example, the South Downs, a rounded upland area of chalk, reach the sea at Beachy Head forming tall white cliffs. The North Downs form the white cliffs of Dover.

chemical weathering: break-up of rock in the place where it lies by chemical processes such as *solution*.

▥ In chemical weathering, the composition of the rock is changed. For example, solution changes limestone (calcium carbonate) into calcium bicarbonate, which is soluble and easily washed away.

cliff: steep rock outcrop along a coast.

▥ A cliff is formed by the action of *destructive waves*. Many cliffs are vertical rock faces. There are several stages in the formation of cliffs:

(1) The bottom of the rock outcrop between high and low water is attacked by destructive waves.

(2) These waves erode the rock by processes such as *abrasion* and *hydraulic action*.

(3) Undercutting at the base of the cliff creates a wave-cut notch.

(4) The rock face above is left overhanging.

(5) Eventually the overhanging rock collapses and the cliff retreats inland.

climate: average weather conditions recorded at a place over many years.

■ Climate is a *physical factor*. Usually, weather observations need to be taken for at least 30 years for the average to be reliable. Temperature and levels of *precipitation* are used to describe a climate.

■ *e.g.* The climate of Britain can be described as cool and wet. Places around the equator have a climate which is hot and wet. The climate of countries around the Mediterranean Sea is characterised by hot, dry summers and warm, wet winters.

coastal protection: human action designed to stop coastal *erosion*.

■ Coastal protection is most necessary where *cliffs* are crumbling because they are made of soft rocks. Methods of coastal protection include sea walls, *groynes* and *gabions*. This is an example of the *management* of a natural environment.

cold front: dividing line between cold and warm air, where the warm air is forced to rise rapidly.

■ A cold front forms at the back of a *depression*. The cooling of air as it rises leads to cloud and rain. The rain is often heavy, sometimes accompanied by thunder and lightning. After a cold front passes, warm air at the surface is replaced by cold air and the temperature falls.

commercial farming: type of agriculture based on growing crops or rearing animals for sale.

■ A commercial farm is run as a business. Money from selling farm produce is used to pay for the *inputs* into the farm, such as labour and fertilisers. In *MEDCs* almost all farming is commercial. The most widespread type of commercial farming in *LEDCs* is *plantation* farming.

Common Agricultural Policy (CAP): system which organises farming within the *European Union*.

■ The Common Agricultural Policy aims to ensure that there is sufficient food for everyone in the EU. It also aims to make the EU as self-sufficient as possible, producing as many different types of food as it can. The CAP works through different types of policy:

● There are fixed prices for many types of farm produce. For some foods, farmers receive a guaranteed price even when the food is in surplus. Surpluses are bought up by the EU and stored.

- Quotas are set up to control over-production, such as milk quotas.
- Farmers are given subsidies to grow crops which will save on imports. For example, growing oil seed rape reduces imports of palm oil from tropical countries. Until self-sufficiency in oil seeds was reached in 1996, the growing of oil seed rape was subsidised.
- Farmers are given grants and loans to buy new machinery and improve the land so that more can be grown.
- To reduce surpluses, farmers have been paid to stop growing crops on some of their land. This policy is known as *set-aside*.

Arguments in favour of the CAP

- food production has increased
- farming is more intensive and more food is produced from the land
- the EU is almost self-sufficient in food
- many more farmers have been able to stay in business than would have been possible without the EU's financial help

Arguments against the CAP

- food prices are higher in Europe than in most other parts of the world
- problems with surpluses remain, such as 'grain mountains' and 'wine lakes'
- it is a very complicated policy which costs millions of euros to administer; money is lost by fraud and fiddling

commuter: person who travels to work every day by car or by public transport.

Commuters do not live in the place where they work. Movements of commuters lead to morning and evening rush hours. As urban areas spread outwards, people need to travel longer distances from the *suburbs* into city centres. Some people move out of urban areas into rural areas and travel to work from a *dormitory settlement*.

commuter settlement: see *dormitory settlement*.

comparison goods: goods which are expensive and bought less frequently.

Comparison goods are *high-order* goods like clothes and jewellery. Many are sold in city centre shops. They are called comparison goods because people are prepared to shop around for them and compare them for price and quality. The opposite is *convenience goods*.

composite volcano: tall volcanic cone built of alternate layers of *lava* and ash.

A composite *volcano* has a typical cone shape. Most form near to *destructive plate boundaries*. By repeated eruptions they grow into high mountains.

e.g. Vesuvius in southern Italy and Mount Fuji in Japan.

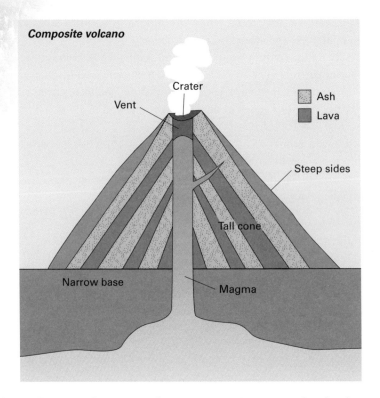

Composite volcano

Crater

Vent

Ash

Lava

Steep sides

Tall cone

Narrow base

Magma

condensation: transformation of water vapour into water droplets by cooling.
- Condensation is one of the processes of the *hydrological cycle*. It takes place when the temperature falls below the *dew-point* of water vapour. Condensation is responsible for the formation of clouds in the sky.

conservation: protection of the Earth and its resources.
- Conservation involves using the Earth's resources in a *sustainable* way. By doing this, resources will be maintained for use by future generations.
- *e.g.* Large-scale conservation projects include:
- reducing consumption of *fossil fuels* and using sources of *alternative energy*
- reducing consumption of *non-renewable resources,* e.g. recycling aluminium cans reduces the amount of bauxite mined
- stopping the destruction of *ecosystems* such as *tropical rainforests* and wetlands
- conserving *biodiversity* by protecting forests, e.g. by turning them into *National Parks*

conservative plate boundary: place where two rock *plates* are moving past each other.
- At a conservative plate boundary, plates meet without the gain or loss of land. This is rarely a smooth process and the region is prone to *earthquakes*.
- *e.g.* The San Andreas fault in California marks the conservative plate boundary between the Pacific and American plates. Both plates are moving towards the

northwest, but at different speeds. They keep locking together. Pressure builds up and is later released as an earthquake shock.

constructive plate boundary (also called 'divergent plate boundary'): place where two rock *plates* are moving away from each other.

▨ At a constructive plate boundary, the gap created by the diverging plates is filled by molten *magma* from the Earth's interior. The magma spreads outwards and forms new crust. This process often takes place on the seafloor to create a *mid-ocean ridge*. The diagram below shows the constructive plate boundary responsible for the mid-Atlantic ridge.

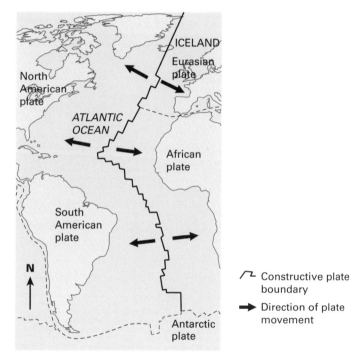

constructive wave: gently breaking wave with a strong *swash* and weak *backwash*, encouraging *deposition*.

▨ Only between six and nine constructive waves break on the shoreline per minute. They are low waves which break forward. This causes a strong swash which carries sand and shingle up the beach. A weak backwash means that only some of this sand and shingle is taken back into the sea. This leads to the accumulation of sand and shingle, and to the formation of landforms of coastal deposition, such as beaches and *spits*. The opposite is a *destructive wave*.

conurbation: large urban area formed by cities growing outwards.

▨ Conurbations swallow up smaller settlements and the countryside around them.

▨ *e.g.* The largest conurbation in the UK is Greater London.

C

convectional rainfall: *precipitation*, often heavy, formed by currents of hot air rising from heated surfaces.

▪ The formation of convectional rainfall begins when *convection currents* rise into the atmosphere. The hot air currents cool as they rise, until water vapour reaches its *dew-point* and *condensation* occurs forming tall *cumulus clouds*. Droplets of water collide in the clouds and increase in size until they are too heavy to be held. Then they fall as rain. Heavy rainfall may be accompanied by thunder, lightning and hail stones. In the tropics, convectional rainfall is the most common type of rain.

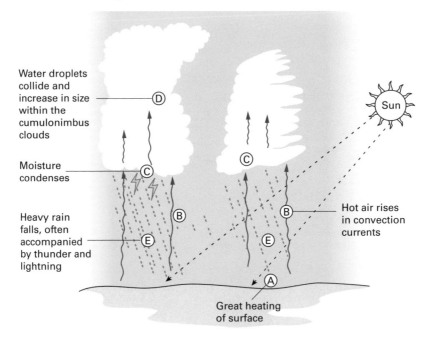

Water droplets collide and increase in size within the cumulonimbus clouds — (D)

Moisture condenses — (C)

Heavy rain falls, often accompanied by thunder and lightning — (E)

(C)

(B) (B)

(E)

(A)

Sun

Hot air rises in convection currents

Great heating of surface

convection current: rising current of air caused by great surface heating.

▪ Air that is heated is lighter and less dense. Surface heating is greatest in the tropics and in inland areas in summer. In these places, currents of air can rise to high levels in the atmosphere. *Condensation* eventually occurs, forming tall *cumulus clouds* and causing *convectional rainfall*.

convenience goods: goods which are cheap and bought frequently.

▪ Most are *low order* goods, such as bread and milk, which are bought close to where a person lives or works. People are unwilling to travel great distances to buy such low value, everyday goods. The opposite is *comparison goods*.

convergent plate boundary: see *destructive plate boundary*.

core: area in the centre or of greatest economic importance.

▪ One part of a country usually becomes richer than the rest. In many countries the core is the name given to the area around the *capital city*. Modern offices, industries and transport services are concentrated here. The opposite of core is *periphery*.

■ *e.g.* The southeast is the core region of the UK. In France it is the Paris region. In Brazil it is the 'Triangulo' in the southeast between São Paulo, Rio de Janeiro and Belo Horizonte. In many smaller *LEDCs* it is the capital city, such as Lima in Peru.

corrasion: see *abrasion.*

corrie: circular hollow high on a mountain side formed by glacial *erosion.*
■ A corrie has a steep and rocky backwall and sides. The front is open, with a rock lip at the end. The hollow is a natural catchment area for water and often contains a small round lake, known as a *tarn lake*. A corrie is the place where snow accumulates to form a *glacier*. In the Alps, corries are called cirques because of their circular shape.

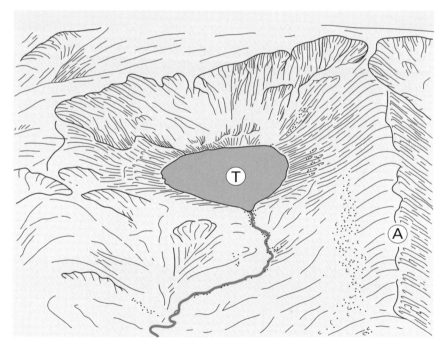

exam watch

Question: *Describe the physical features of the corrie shown in the sketch.*
Answer: The backwall and sides of the corrie are steep. A narrow ridge marked by the letter A is found on one side. This is likely to be an *arête*. There are loose rocks, which could be *scree*, at the bottom of this ridge. The corrie is hollow in the centre and is filled by a small circular lake. This is a tarn lake (T). A stream can be seen running out of the front of the lake.

Question: *Explain the formation of a corrie.*

Answer: Frost action on the mountains above the corrie and on the backwall breaks off pieces of rock. Ice sticking to the headwall pulls away blocks of rock by plucking as the glacier moves. The loose rocks from frost action and plucking are embedded in the bottom of the ice and become tools for abrasion. Pressure from erosion is greatest at the bottom of the headwall due to the rotational movement of the ice. A deep hollow is formed at the back. Where the erosion is less powerful, a rock lip forms at the front.

corrosion: breakdown of rocks by chemical action.

■ *Carboniferous limestone* is affected by limestone *solution*, a type of *chemical weathering*. It contributes to erosion by rivers and waves in areas of limestone rocks.

crater: circular hole at the top of a volcanic cone.

■ A crater is located at the top of the *vent* in the centre of a *volcano*. *Lava*, ash, gases and dust are erupted from here. These erupted materials build up around the sides of the crater, making volcanoes cone-shaped.

cumulus clouds: tall clouds which sometimes give rise to heavy rain.

■ *Convection currents* of hot air rise high into the sky. *Condensation* occurs and clouds form. When cumulus clouds continue to grow into towering cumulo-nimbus, thunder and lightning and heavy downpours of rain occur.

cyclone: see *hurricane*.

dam: concrete structure retaining water in a lake or *reservoir*.

■ Small dams are mainly used for supplying water to towns and cities. Large dams are normally multi-purpose (built for several purposes) and may be used for water supply, *hydroelectric power*, *irrigation*, river *management* and *flood* prevention.

■ *e.g.* The Aswan High Dam is a multi-purpose dam on the River Nile in Egypt.

Arguments in favour of dam building

- **social** — the quality of life of local people is improved by supplies of clean water and electricity
- **economic** — water can be used for irrigating crops which results in a higher output; hydroelectric power provides electricity for use in factories
- **environmental** — hydroelectric power is a clean source of energy which doesn't pollute the atmosphere like *fossil fuels*
- **political** — the government is increasing the country's level of economic *development*

Arguments against dam building

- **social** — people may be forced to move from their homes to allow the land behind the dam to be flooded
- **economic** — electricity from hydroelectric power may be supplied to people living many kilometres away in large cities, rather than the local people
- **environmental** — wildlife habitats are destroyed and some animals may drown when the land is flooded
- **political** — less water is left in the river for people in the next country downstream

death rate: number of deaths per 1,000 people per year.

■ The average death rate is 10 per 1,000 in *MEDCs* and 9 per 1,000 in *LEDCs*. Death rates have fallen rapidly all over the world during the last 50 years as a result of the spread of improved medical knowledge. Only a few very poor African countries, such as Rwanda and Sierra Leone which have wars and high levels of disease, have a death rate above 20 per 1,000. Although medical facilities, access to clean water and diet are better in MEDCs than in LEDCs, MEDCs also have an *ageing population* which stops the death rate falling any lower. In LEDCs there is a much higher percentage of young people under 16, which also keeps the death rate low. However, death rates are increasing in those African countries badly affected by HIV and AIDs, such as Zimbabwe and Botswana.

debt: money owed to others.

■ Many *LEDCs* have a debt problem and owe money to governments or banks in other countries. This has become a major international issue. In the past, governments in LEDCs borrowed money to try to develop their countries economically. Now many cannot even afford to pay back the interest on the loans and the debts are increasing. As a result, some African and South American countries are becoming poorer rather than developing economically.

deforestation: cutting down trees and clearing forests.

■ Deforestation is a controversial issue (see *tropical rainforests*). Some governments, in countries such as Brazil, wish to use more of their *natural resources* and open up larger areas to settlement and *development*. Other people argue that deforestation has serious local and global consequences for the environment because forests:
- reduce *runoff* and *floods*
- use up carbon dioxide from the atmosphere
- maintain the Earth's *biodiversity*

delta: landform created where a river splits up and flows in several channels or *distributaries*.

■ A delta is a landform of river *deposition*. It is built up of great thicknesses of *silt*. Most are triangular-shaped areas of land, extending into the sea. The land between the channels is low lying and flat.

Big rivers, such as the Nile (see opposite) and Ganges, form deltas where they meet the sea. This is because these rivers:
- transport large *loads*
- are slow flowing
- meet denser salt water that holds back their flow

Deltas build up fastest where sea currents and tides are weak, such as in the Mediterranean Sea. The Mississippi carries such a massive load of sediment that it has built up a bird's foot delta, in which lines of sediment extend out to sea along the sides of each of its distributaries.

Delta regions are challenging places for people to live. These areas are among the first to be flooded by rising sea levels. On the other hand, the silt soils are incredibly fertile and easy to work. The Nile delta in Egypt and the Ganges delta in Bangladesh are two of the world's most densely populated rural areas.

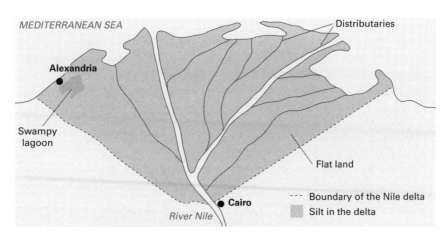

demographic transition model: line graph showing the relationship between a country's *birth rate* and *death rate* over time.

■ The difference between the lines indicates the rate of *natural increase*. The model is divided into four main stages. As a country develops economically, it passes further through the stages. All countries have moved out of stage 1. *LEDCs* are in stages 2 and 3. *MEDCs* are in stage 4.

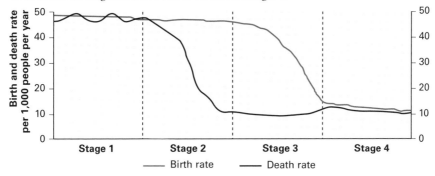

Stage	Birth rate	Death rate	Natural increase	Example
1	High	High	Low	Subsistence groups, e.g. tribes of Indians in the Amazon Basin
2	High	Decreasing	Increasing	LEDCs with low levels of economic development, e.g. Mali (birth rate 50, death rate 18)
3	Decreasing	Low	Decreasing	LEDCs with increasing levels of economic development, e.g. Mexico (birth rate 25, death rate 5)
4	Low	Low	Low	MEDCs, e.g. UK (birth rate 12, death rate 11)

Summary of stages in the demographic transition model

dependant: person of non-working age.
 There are two main groups of dependants:
 • children under 15 years
 • people above retirement age (on average 65 years)
 Dependants have to be supported by those of working age. For example, under-15s need education and over-65s need pensions.

dependency ratio: relationship between the percentage of working age people and the percentage of non-working age people.
 The higher the percentage of working age people (15–65 years), the more income is being produced for a country to support those of non-working ages (under 15 and over 65 years).

deposition: laying down of sediments which accumulate and build *landforms*.
 Rivers, waves and glaciers erode and transport sediment. This sediment is dropped when it can no longer be carried and builds up with time.
 River deposition — rivers deposit where their speed of flow is reduced. This is often in their lower course where the gradient is less. Landforms created by river deposition include *slip-off slopes* on the inside of *meanders, levées, floodplains* and *deltas*. River sediment is called *alluvium*.
 Coastal deposition — waves deposit at a bend in the coastline or in locations where *constructive waves* are most likely. Landforms created by coastal deposition include *beaches, spits* and *bars*. Sand, shingle and pebbles are the main sediments deposited.
 Glacial deposition — glaciers deposit across lowlands where the ice is melting and becoming thinner. Landforms created by glacial deposition include *drumlins* and *moraines*. *Boulder clay* is the main deposit.

depression: area of *low pressure* in *temperate latitudes*, such as the British Isles.
 A depression is associated with a *warm front* and a *cold front*, where warm air meets cold air. The lighter warm air rises, which leads to areas of lower than average surface pressure. As it rises, the air cools and *condensation* occurs to form a band of rain along the fronts. The weather can be summarised as cloudy, wet and windy. The opposite of a depression is an *anticyclone*.

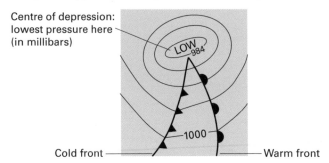

How a depression looks on a weather map

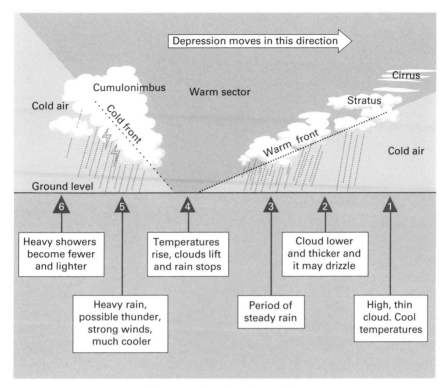

Cross-section of a depression

desert: area of low *precipitation*, under 250 mm per year.

⬛ Hot deserts are found in the tropics. Most of the surface consists of sand, stones and bare rock.

⬛ *e.g.* The largest hot desert is the Sahara in Africa.

Deserts are permanently dry places. They must not be confused with areas suffering from *drought*, which are unexpectedly dry.

desertification: spread of *desert*, mainly as a result of human actions.

⬛ Human actions which lead to desertification include chopping down trees, collecting fuelwood, population increase (which increases demand for food production), *overgrazing* and overcultivation. Several areas of the world are affected, but the main one is the Sahel region on the southern edges of the Sahara Desert, shown overleaf. The impact of human activities has been made worse by many years of lower than average rainfall.

Desertification is a serious environmental problem. Once grasses and bushes are removed, and the land can no longer be cultivated, the bare surface is exposed to *soil erosion* by wind and water. It is also a serious human problem, creating the danger of *famine*, as in Ethiopia.

exam watch

23

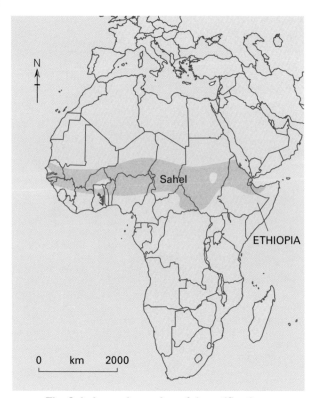

The Sahel, a major region of desertification

destructive plate boundary (also called 'convergent plate boundary'): place where two rock *plates* move towards each other and collide.

■ At a destructive plate boundary, one plate is destroyed as it sinks below the other into a *subduction zone*. As this happens, the crust melts and *magma* rises to the surface and forms *volcanoes*. The great movement of rock against rock causes *earthquakes*. As the plates collide, sediments are compressed up into *fold mountains*.

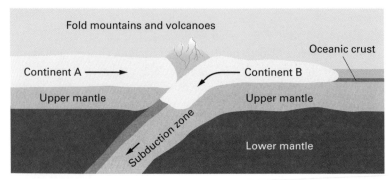

■ *e.g.* The Nazca plate sinks below the South American plate off the west coast of South America.

destructive wave: powerful wave with weak *swash* and a strong *backwash*, encouraging *erosion*.

▨ Destructive waves break frequently: there are between 12 and 15 of them per minute. They are high waves with a circular motion, which causes a strong backwash. The backwash carries pebbles and shingle out to sea and is the reason why destructive waves cause coastal erosion. They speed up the retreat of *cliffs* by undercutting them at their base and removing rocks after they have been broken off. The opposite is a *constructive wave*.

development: level of economic growth and wealth of a country.

▨ In terms of economic development, the world is usually split into two parts, divided by a line which separates more economically developed countries (*MEDCs*) from less economically developed countries (*LEDCs*).

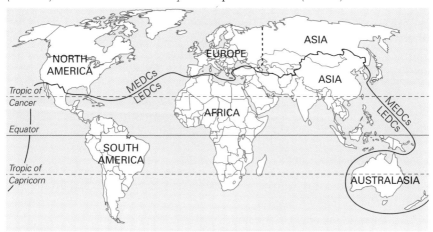

Higher levels of economic development mean greater wealth for a country and its people. The differences between LEDCs and MEDCs, which result from their different levels of economic development, are summarised below.

	LEDCs	MEDCs
Economic	Low GDP per head (often below US$1,000)	High GDP per head (many above US$10,000)
	High percentage work in farming (often over 40% of workers)	High percentage work in services (usually over 50% of workers)
Social	Low life expectancy (in some countries less than 50 years)	High life expectancy (usually above 70 years)
	Low literacy levels (over 50% illiterate, especially women)	High literacy levels (almost 100%)
	High birth rates and natural increase (birth rate over 25, natural increase over 2%)	Low birth rates and natural increase (birth rate under 13, natural increase less than 0.5%)

dew: moisture on the ground formed by *condensation* of water vapour.

▨ Dew forms when the ground becomes colder than the air above. This usually happens at night when skies are clear and there is little or no wind. Water vapour in the air is cooled below its *dew-point* and condenses to form water droplets on the ground. This is why the grass is wet on summer mornings during spells of fine weather.

dew-point: temperature at which *condensation* occurs, transforming water vapour into water droplets.

▨ The dew-point temperature can be reached in the atmosphere as air rises and cools. This causes clouds to form. It can also be reached on the ground during nights with clear skies when heat escapes into space. This causes dew to form.

discharge: volume of water flowing in a river per second.

▨ Discharge is measured in cubic metres per second. It is calculated by the formula: cross-sectional area × velocity of water.

distributary: smaller river channel that has split from the main river channel.

▨ Distributaries get their name because water in the river, instead of flowing in one channel, is distributed in separate channels. For example, each channel in a *delta* is a distributary. A distributary must not be confused with a *tributary*.

divergent plate boundary: see *constructive plate boundary*.

diversification: moving into new business activities to widen the range of products and sources of income.

▨ Many companies diversify in the hope that decline in one activity will be offset by increase in another.

▨ *e.g.* Because incomes from farming are falling in the European Union, some farmers have explored new ways of making money, such as farm shops, bed and breakfast and forestry.

dormant: describes a *volcano* that is no longer active but which might erupt again in the future.

▨ Most volcanoes 'sleep' between periods of great activity.

dormitory settlement (also called 'commuter settlement')**:** village or small town where many residents travel to work elsewhere.

▨ A dormitory settlement is often a small, attractive place. People choose to live there for peace and quiet. There is little work in the village, so people must travel to places of work in towns and cities. These people are known as *commuters*. A dormitory settlement needs to have good transport links to larger settlements.

drainage basin: area of land drained by a river and its tributaries.

▨ Within the area of a drainage basin all *rainfall* and surface *runoff* makes its way into the main river. The edge of the drainage basin is marked by higher land. It is separated from surrounding river basins by the highest land, known as the *watershed*.

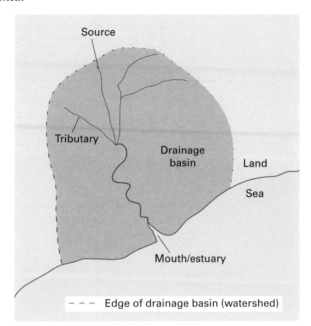

— — — Edge of drainage basin (watershed)

drought: period of dry weather beyond that normally expected.

▦ Lack of water causes many problems, such as:

- reduced crop yields
- shortage of good grazing
- falling water levels in reservoirs

One of the worst affected areas over the last 30 years has been the Sahel region of Africa, where *desertification* and *famine* have been major problems.

The term drought is not used to describe conditions in an area which is permanently dry and in which little rain is ever expected, such as a *desert*.

drumlin: egg-shaped mound of *boulder clay*.

▦ A drumlin is a landform of glacial *deposition*. It is a low hill, up to 150 m high and 500 m long. Often a number of drumlins are found in the same lowland area. The undulating land surface that results is known as 'basket of eggs topography'.

▦ *e.g.* Drumlins are numerous in northwest England, such as around the edges of the Lake District, where faster ice flows moulded the boulder clay into this shape.

dry point site: settlement placed on land which is free from flooding.
■ Villages are often sited on the lower slopes of a valley or on a small hill.

dry valley: *V-shaped valley* without a stream flowing in the bottom of it.
■ Dry valleys are most common in areas of *chalk*. Instead of flowing across the surface, rainwater seeps underground to fill the spaces in the chalk. The valleys were eroded in earlier times when surface streams were present. This could have been at the end of an *ice age* when there were massive amounts of surface meltwater.

earthquake: shaking of the ground surface.

▥ The shaking is greatest at the *epicentre*, the point on the surface directly above the earthquake's source. There are thousands of earthquakes in the world each year. Most of them happen on and near *plate* boundaries. Many of the strongest earthquakes occur along *destructive plate boundaries*, where there is great friction caused by a rock plate sinking and being destroyed. The strength of an earthquake is measured on the *Richter scale*. Although areas at risk from earthquakes are well known, it is impossible to predict when one will occur.

Immediate effects of earthquakes
- injuries and fatalities
- collapsed buildings
- destruction of roads, bridges and power lines

Short-term effects of earthquakes
- injured people requiring treatment
- people trapped in rubble
- shortage of medical supplies, food, clean water and shelter
- danger of disease spreading

Long-term effects of earthquakes
- homelessness, people living in temporary shelters or camps
- poverty resulting from lack of work and essential services
- cost of rebuilding bridges, roads and buildings

exam watch

economic factor: factor related to money or wealth.

ecosystem: system where living things (plants and animals) and physical factors (climate and soils) are linked.

▥ *Climate* greatly affects the type of *natural vegetation* which grows in an area. The vegetation, in turn, affects the area's animal life. In an ecosystem, changes to one element affect all the others. For example, when the natural vegetation is cleared, climate, soil and animal life are all affected.

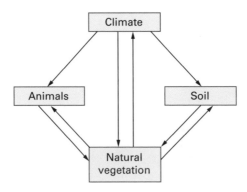

The structure of an ecosystem

ecotourism (also known as 'green tourism')**:** type of tourism which involves protecting the environment and the way of life of local people.

■ Maintaining places and environments for ecotourism requires *management,* as in a *National Park.* Local people are given opportunities to earn income from visitors by providing some of the services needed.

emigration: movement of people from one country to another.

■ Emigration is international *migration.* Some emigration is voluntary. For example, people emigrate from Mexico to the USA looking for work, or work with higher pay. Some emigration is forced. People may be forced to flee from a country because of war, persecution or political unrest. These people are *refugees.*

energy: factor such as electricity or fuel, needed for work to be done.

■ In general, the higher a country's level of economic *development,* the greater its use of energy. The amount of energy used in the world continues to increase. Most energy still comes from *fossil fuels,* such as oil and coal, which are *non-renewable resources.* Only a small proportion is *alternative energy,* e.g. *hydroelectric power* and *wind power,* which comes from *renewable resources.*

enterprise zone: area of Britain in which businesses can receive financial help from the government.

■ Some enterprise zones are in areas of high unemployment. Others are in areas where the land is derelict and in need of redevelopment. The financial help is designed to attract new business. For example, businesses in an enterprise zone may be exempted from paying rates for 10 years.

■ *e.g.* The London Docklands and the MetroCentre (shopping centre) in Gateshead are both large-scale, successful developments which began in enterprise zones. Both are located on the banks of rivers where shipping had declined.

epicentre: point on the Earth's surface directly above the source of an *earthquake.*

All earthquakes begin at a point underground known as the 'focus'. The epicentre is directly above the focus and is where the earthquake shaking is greatest. The further the distance from the epicentre, the weaker the shock waves become.

equator: latitude 0°.

The equator is the imaginary line around the middle of the earth which is an equal distance from both poles. It divides the world into the northern and southern hemispheres.

equatorial climate: hot, wet climate found in lowland areas within 10° of the equator.

An equatorial climate is hot all year because the sun is always at a high angle in the sky (high rates of *insolation*). It is wet all year because *convection currents* rise from the heated ground to produce heavy *convectional rainfall*. This climate provides ideal conditions for plant growth, giving rise to *tropical rainforest* vegetation.

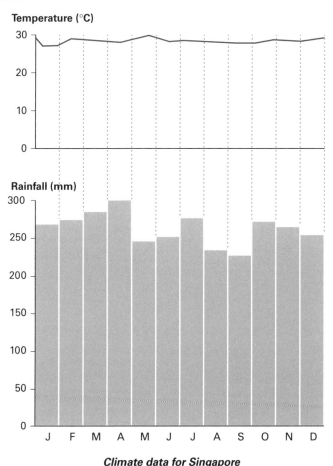

Climate data for Singapore

Question: *Describe the temperature.*
Your answer should give the:
- highest temperature
- lowest temperature
- annual range of temperature
- shape of the line

Question: *Describe the precipitation.*
Your answer should give the:
- month with the highest amount
- time of year when most precipitation falls
- general pattern

erosion: wearing away of the Earth's surface by rivers, glaciers, waves and wind.

Rivers, ice, sea and wind are known as 'agents of erosion'. Each one wears away surface rocks by movement. Some of the rocks may have already been loosened by *weathering*. The combined effect of weathering and erosion is to wear away the rocks on the Earth's surface. There are many processes of erosion:
- river erosion — *abrasion, attrition, corrosion, hydraulic action*
- glacial erosion — abrasion, *plucking*
- coastal erosion — abrasion, attrition, corrosion, hydraulic action
- wind erosion — abrasion, attrition

There is a continuous cycle of erosion and mountain-building in the world.

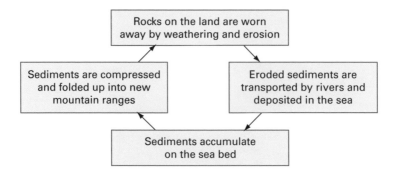

erratic: boulder dropped by a *glacier*, of a different type from the rock below it.

escarpment: upland landform with one slope noticeably steeper than the other.

The short, steep slope is a scarp slope. The long, gentle slope is a dip slope. This landform is most characteristic of *chalk* areas in southern England. The chalk resists *erosion* more than the weaker clay which surrounds it. An escarpment has distinctive patterns of land use and settlement, as summarised on the cross-section opposite.

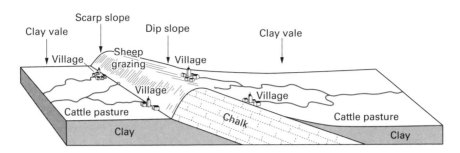

estuary: *mouth* of a river where the channel is wide and tidal.

▨ There is only one river channel in an estuary (compared with many river channels, or *distributaries*, in a *delta*). At low tide, large areas of mud and saltmarsh are exposed. Deep and wide estuaries, such as the Thames estuary, can be used by shipping.

EU: see *European Union*.

European Union (EU): organisation which links together 15 European countries.

▨ The European Union began as the 'Common Market' for goods and services. Removal of all barriers to *trade* between member countries was of greatest importance. The EU is administered from Brussels. There are economic policies for agriculture, industry, fishing and regional assistance, such as the *Common Agricultural Policy*. There are also social policies and laws in other areas, such as employment rights. The 15 member countries are Austria, Belgium, Denmark, Eire (the Irish Republic), Finland, France, Germany, Greece, Italy, Luxembourg, the Netherlands, Portugal, Spain, Sweden and the UK.

evaporation: transformation of water droplets into water vapour by heating.

▨ Heat causes water surfaces to give off water vapour into the air. Evaporation is one of the processes in the *hydrological cycle*.

evapotranspiration: loss of water from a *drainage basin* into the atmosphere from plants and all other sources.

▨ Evapotranspiration is a combination of two processes, *evaporation* and *transpiration*. It is often difficult to separate out water losses from different sources. The rate of evapotranspiration increases in high temperatures and strong winds. Evapotranspiration is one of the processes in the *hydrological cycle*.

export: sale of goods and services to other countries.

▨ This is *trade* with other countries in order to earn income. Foreign exchange is earned which can be used to *import* goods and services from other countries. There are two groups of exports:

● visible exports — goods which can be measured, weighed or counted, such as bananas, cars and iron-ore

- invisible exports — services sold to another country, such as tourism and banking (see *invisible trade*)

extensive farming: type of agriculture producing a low output per hectare from large areas of land.

■ *Inputs* are low but so are *outputs*.

■ **e.g.** hill sheep farming in areas such as the Lake District. Each sheep needs a large area because most of the land is *rough grazing*. Cattle ranching in Australia is also extensive. Cattle are left to graze wide areas with little input from farmers.

factory: place where *raw materials* are processed and made into different products.

factory farming: type of agriculture based on intensive rearing of animals, usually indoors.
■ The animals are reared as if they were part of a factory production line. They are fed on a controlled diet for fastest growth. Farming by these methods has helped to keep food prices low. However, some people object to the methods used, especially when the animals are kept indoors in confined spaces. Disease also spreads more quickly. Factory farming methods for keeping pigs have been abandoned for these reasons. Most pigs are now kept in fields where they can root around in a more natural way. Costs of producing pork have increased.

factory system: *inputs*, processes and *outputs* which change *raw materials* into finished products.

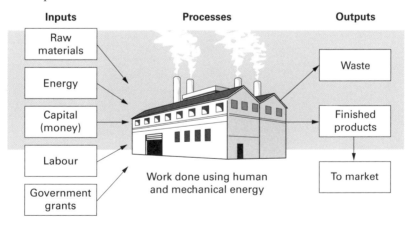

famine: serious shortage of food causing people to become very ill or die.
■ Parts of Africa, especially countries in the Sahel such as Ethiopia, have been badly affected in the recent past. *Drought* is the main cause of famine. However, human factors make the situation worse. These include:

- *natural increase* in population — this creates more mouths to feed
- *overgrazing* and overcultivation — farmers trying to increase food output may ruin farmland
- war — this disrupts farming and makes it difficult to bring in supplies of food from elsewhere

farm system: *inputs*, processes and *outputs* for growing crops and breeding livestock.

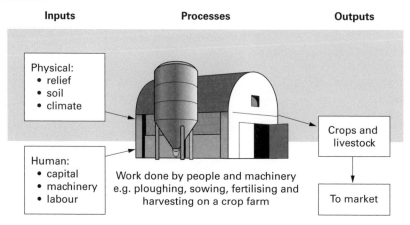

fault: vertical fracture which breaks up a bed of rock.

■ Before faulting, the bed of rock is in one continuous section. After faulting, beds are broken by fractures.

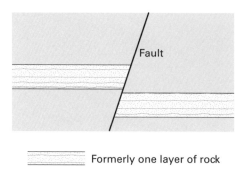

Faults are formed by earth movements which cause beds of rock to be moved up or down. Large-scale faulting may form a *rift valley*.

fertiliser: manure or chemicals added to soil to increase output.

■ Fertiliser is one of the *inputs* associated with *intensive farming*. Fertilisers replace nutrients taken out of the soil by crops in previous years. They improve the yield of a crop per hectare. Manure is an organic fertiliser which also improves the soil structure. Inorganic fertilisers can cause environmental damage when they are washed out of the soil into streams.

fertility rate: average number of children born to a woman in her lifetime.

▨ The higher a country's fertility rate, the higher its *birth rate* and in general the higher its rate of *natural increase*. In many *MEDCs*, fertility rates are below 2.0. In the UK the rate is 1.8. However, it is only 1.2 in Spain and Italy, two countries which now have a *natural decrease* in population. The average fertility rate in *LEDCs* is 3.1 but there are wide variations. Fertility rates above 5.0 are common in countries in Africa and the Middle East.

fjord: drowned, glaciated valley, usually long and deep with steep sides.

▨ Fjords are some of the world's deepest inlets and best natural harbours. They were formed by powerful glaciers eroding *U-shaped valleys* in mountainous coastal areas like Norway. Rising sea levels after the *ice age* flooded the bottoms of the valleys.

flood: temporary excess of water which covers land areas that are usually dry.

▨ Flooding by rivers is normal. It is part of the annual pattern of *discharge*. *Floodplains* could not form without regular river floods. Floods also affect low-lying coastal areas, such as the Netherlands. River *management* is used to reduce the risk of floods and lessen their effects.

▨ *e.g.* Large areas of land were under water in the UK during the wet autumn and winter of 2000–01.

Natural causes
- wet season with prolonged and heavy rainfall
- melting of snow and ice in the mountains during spring and summer
- torrential downpour, such as a tropical hurricane or a thunderstorm

Human causes
- deforestation leading to greater and faster *runoff*
- building urban areas — hard surfaces and drains increase the speed of runoff
- occasional disasters, such as a dam burst
- building more houses in high-risk areas, such as on floodplains

floodplain: flat land on the sides of a river, usually in its lower course.

▨ A floodplain is a landform of river *deposition*. It is built up from great thicknesses of *silt* deposited every time the river floods. It is widened by lateral *erosion* on the outside bends of *meanders* where they touch the sides of the floodplain.

fodder crop: crop grown by a farmer for feeding to livestock.

▨ Animals kept and fed indoors need fodder. In the UK, grass is dried as hay or made into silage to be fed to livestock during winter.

fog: cloud at ground level, reducing visibility to less than 1 kilometre.

▨ Fog forms when *condensation* takes place close to the ground surface. When skies are clear, heat is lost and the ground becomes cold. The cold ground cools the air above by contact, and water vapour condenses into water droplets. In lowland areas, especially in valley floors, fog is most likely to form on winter nights. Low cloud often creates hill fog in upland areas, so that the tops of the hills cannot be seen.

folding: bending of layers of rock due to earth movements, creating upfolds and downfolds.

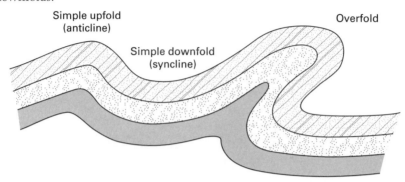

fold mountains: long, high mountain range formed by the upfolding of sediments by powerful earth movements.

■ Fold mountains form at *destructive plate boundaries*. As the two rock plates collide, sediments that had accumulated on the sea bed are compressed. They are forced upwards in a series of great folds.

■ *e.g.* the Rockies, Andes, Alps and Himalayas.

footloose industry: industry which has great freedom of choice of location.

■ Many are *light industries* or *high-tech industries* which do not need bulky raw materials or a lot of energy. The opposite is *heavy industry*. Footloose industries have the freedom to pick locations which best suit them. Factors **most** likely to influence choice of location include:
- transport — access to motorways (the M4 and M11 corridors have attracted many footloose industries) and airports
- *market* — proximity to places where many people live, possibly with high spending power
- *greenfield sites* — near to pleasant countryside
  Factors **least** likely to influence choice of location include:
- *raw materials* — only needed in small amounts
- *energy* supplies — electricity is available everywhere

fossil fuel: energy source from plants and animals that died millions of years ago.

■ Coal, oil and natural gas are the three main types of fossil fuel. All are *non-renewable resources*, having taken millions of years to form. Fossil fuels are easy to use. However, burning them leads to atmospheric *pollution*, such as *acid rain*, and *global warming*. They are being used up at a faster rate than new sources are being formed. The world relies upon fossil fuels for 75% of its energy needs.

Fossil fuel	Life expectancy in 2000 (years)	World energy use in 2000 (%)
Coal	230	21
Oil	41	34
Natural gas	62	20

fragile environment: natural environment that can easily be damaged by the actions of people.
- The most fragile environments are those where physical conditions allow only slow growth, such as *tundra* regions in the Arctic. The tundra climate is cold and summers are very short. Only small plants can grow, and these can easily be damaged.

freeze–thaw: frost action leading to the break-up of rock.
- Freeze–thaw is a type of *physical weathering*. Temperatures must go above and below freezing point regularly for it to occur. When the temperature drops below freezing, water trapped in cracks in the rock freezes and expands. This puts pressure on the surrounding rock. Thawing releases the pressure. After freezing and thawing has been repeated many times, sharp-edged pieces of rock are broken off, known as *scree*. Freeze–thaw occurs most regularly in mountainous areas and polar lands.

front: dividing line between different air masses, where air is rising.
- The different types of front are named according to the temperature of the air which follows behind as the front passes over a place. A *warm front* brings warm air after it passes through. A *cold front* brings cold air and lower temperatures. Fronts are part of mid-latitude *depressions*.

frontal rainfall: *precipitation* caused by the passage of a *warm front* and a *cold front* in a *depression*.
- At a front, warm air is forced to rise over cold air. As it rises it cools, dew-point is reached, *condensation* occurs and it rains. Rainfall is often heavier along the cold front where the warm air is forced to rise more strongly.

function: with respect to a settlement, what it does and why it is there.
- Some settlements have one main function. They can be given labels, such as capital city, port, market town, seaside resort or mining village. Large cities have many functions.

gabion: wire basket filled with rocks placed where there is river or coastal *erosion*.
- Gabions are a method of river or coastal *management* to reduce rates of erosion. In river channels they protect the outside bends of *meanders*. Along the coast they protect the base of cliffs.

GDP: see *gross domestic product*.

gentrification: movement of wealthy people into an area of former *urban decay*.
- Richer people tend to leave decaying areas of the *inner city* and move to the *suburbs*. However, sometimes old houses are bought up by wealthy people who can afford to improve them. Once this happens to several houses, the residential status of the area improves. Others are willing to move back into the inner city areas.
- *e.g.* Islington and Notting Hill in London.

geothermal power: generating electricity and heat from the ground, usually in volcanic areas.
- Water from natural hot springs can be piped to houses and used directly for hot water and heating. Greater heat is needed to generate electricity. Water from the surface is sent underground to be heated by the hot rocks. It is pumped back to the surface where it drives generators in geothermal power stations. This is clean, *alternative energy* from a *renewable resource*.
- *e.g.* Most houses in Iceland are heated using geothermal energy from hot springs. Both Iceland and New Zealand have geothermal power stations.

glaciation: actions and processes associated with *glaciers*.
- A long period of glaciation is known as an *ice age*.

glacier: moving mass of ice in a valley.
- Glaciers form in high mountains where more new snow falls each year than melts. Snow is compressed into ice in a *corrie*. When it is large enough, the glacier spills over the rock lip at the front of the corrie and follows a pre-existing river valley. As the glacier flows, the valley is changed into a *U-shaped valley*. Eventually, the glacier melts on low ground where temperatures are higher.

globalisation: increasing importance of international operations for people and companies.

▨ Decisions taken by people in one country affect what happens in others. Few people and industries are left untouched by what happens in other countries or other parts of the world. There has been a revolution in global communications. It is easy to communicate with people anywhere in the world by e-mail, phone or fax. Most places in the world can be reached within 24 hours by aeroplane.

It is cheaper to make clothes and shoes in Asia and transport them by container to the UK, than it is to make them in the UK where wage rates are much higher. *Multinational companies* take decisions in their headquarters which have worldwide effects. When directors at Ford and General Motors decide to make fewer cars in the UK, the decision is made in Detroit in the USA, not in the UK.

global warming: rise in average world temperatures.

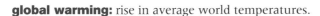

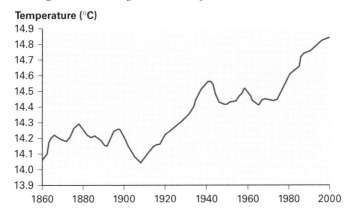

Temperature (°C)

▨ Many believe that humans are to blame for global warming. They claim that the amount of carbon dioxide in the atmosphere is increasing due to *deforestation* and burning of *fossil fuels*. This increases the *greenhouse effect* of the atmosphere, trapping heat from the Earth's surface. Others believe that global warming is a natural process. They point out that climate keeps changing. The Earth has been heating up for the last 10,000 years, since the last *ice age*. The Earth has in the past been warmer than it is today.

Whatever the cause, people in some countries are very worried about the possible effects of global warming which could cause sea levels to rise. Most at risk are people living in low-lying coastal areas, for example parts of eastern England, the Netherlands, the Ganges Delta in Bangladesh and coral islands, such as the Maldives in the Indian Ocean. International conferences in Kyoto in 1997 and The Hague in 2001 discussed strategies for reducing global warming. It was difficult to reach international agreement about how to reduce carbon dioxide emissions and by how much.

g

gorge: narrow valley with rocky sides.

■ A gorge is a landform of river *erosion*. It forms below a *waterfall* where a river has cut down through a hard band of rock. A gorge can also be a feature of *karst* scenery which forms in areas of *Carboniferous limestone* after a *cavern* roof collapses.

green belt: area of land, mainly countryside, around a large town or city.

■ Green belts are protected from urban development. Planning permission for building on such areas will only be allowed in special circumstances. The main purpose of a green belt is to stop the spread of urban areas into surrounding countryside and to stop settlements from joining up to form a *conurbation*. A second purpose is to preserve some open space for recreation.

greenfield site: open land which has never been previously built on.

■ This is rural land around the edges of towns and cities, such as fields and woodland. There is more and more pressure to allow building on such sites for out-of-town supermarkets, shopping centres, *business parks*, factories and new houses. Many businesses prefer these sites because they are often near to motorways and there is plenty of space for car parking. The opposite is a *brownfield site*.

greenhouse effect: the trapping of energy by carbon dioxide and other gases which prevents some of the Earth's surface heat from escaping into space.

■ The process of the greenhouse effect is normal. However, the amount of carbon dioxide and other 'greenhouse' gases (methane, chlorofluorocarbons and nitrous oxide) in the atmosphere has increased. Pollution from burning *fossil fuels* and *deforestation* is thought to be partly responsible. As more heat is now being trapped near the surface, *global warming* is occurring.

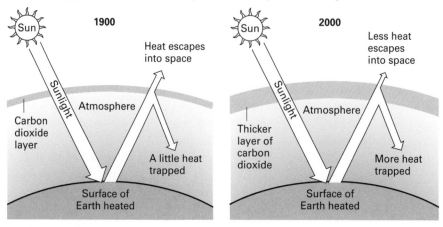

green revolution: large increase in food production in some *LEDCs* since the 1960s following the introduction of new, high-yielding seeds.

■ The *high-yielding varieties* are mainly cereals, such as wheat and rice. Since the green revolution, subsistence farmers in countries such as India have been more able to feed their families and even have surpluses for sale in local markets. However, owners of large farms have benefited most because they can afford the *fertilisers*, pesticides and *irrigation* that enable the highest yields to be obtained from the new seeds.

green tourism: see *ecotourism*.

gross domestic product (GDP): measure of a country's wealth, usually given per head of its population.

■ Gross means total. Domestic product is the value of goods and services produced in a country in 1 year. It is divided by the number of people living in the country to obtain a value per head. The formula is:

$$\text{GDP per person} = \frac{\text{total value of all goods and services produced in a country in a year}}{\text{total population of the country}}$$

It is the best indicator of the relative wealth between different countries. The table below shows GDP per head for several countries in the mid-1990s. For comparison, the UK figure was US$18,620.

Top three wealthiest countries (US$)		Bottom three poorest countries (US$)	
Luxembourg	34,155	Rwanda	352
USA	26,397	Ethiopia	427
Switzerland	24,967	Democratic Republic of the Congo (formerly Zaire)	429

groundwater: water stored underground in *permeable rock*, such as *chalk*.

■ When it rains, *infiltration* occurs and water moves into the ground through the soil. This water is stored in spaces in the rock below the *water table*. Groundwater flows back onto the surface through *springs*, which feed rivers and streams.

groundwater flow: movement of water through soil and rock as a result of gravity.

■ This is one of the processes in the *hydrological cycle*.

growing season: time of year when it is warm enough for crops to grow.

■ A temperature of at least 6°C is needed for grass and other crops to grow. In the tropics the growing season is all year. In cool *temperate latitudes*, as in the UK, the growing season is summer. The growing season becomes shorter from southwest to northeast in the British Isles, ranging from 8–9 months in Cornwall down to 4–5 months north of Inverness. In *tundra* lands, such as in Alaska, the growing season is too short for crops to be planted.

g

groyne: barrier, usually made of wood, running down a beach to trap sand and shingle transported by *longshore drift* along the coast.

Groynes are used to prevent loss of sand from beaches. They are also used for *coastal protection*. If a wide and deep beach can be retained, there is less chance of waves reaching and eroding the cliffs behind.

e.g. Groynes can be seen in UK seaside resorts, such as Bournemouth and Eastbourne.

habitat: home of a living community of plants and animals.

▨ A natural habitat is a place where wildlife continues to live free from major human interference. Wildlife habitats lost in recent years in the UK include hedgerows and wetlands. The clearance of *tropical rainforests* is leading to habitat loss in the Amazon Basin.

hamlet: small *rural settlement.*

▨ A hamlet is a cluster of a few houses and farms without any services. It is at the bottom of the *hierarchy* of settlement.

hanging valley: *tributary* valley which joins a main *U-shaped valley* from a higher level.

▨ A hanging valley is a landform of glacial *erosion*. It forms when a main valley is more greatly eroded by a *glacier* than a tributary valley. This leaves the tributary valley 'hanging' at a higher level than the main valley. After the glaciers melt, the tributary river flows down to the main valley as a *waterfall.*

▨ **e.g.** Lauterbrunnen valley near Interlaken in Switzerland.

hazard: see *natural hazard.*

headland: point along a coastline where rock extends further out into the sea than the rocks on either side.

▨ A headland is a landform of glacial *erosion*. The rock which makes up a headland is harder and more resistant to wave action than the softer rocks around it. Cliffs are always present. Headlands made of *chalk*, such as Flamborough Head, also have *caves*, *arches* and *stacks*.

heavy industry: *manufacturing industry* making large or bulky products, such as ships and steel girders.

▨ The main *inputs* of heavy industry are *raw materials* and *energy*. These are needed in large amounts, which is why heavy industries are most commonly located:

• next to sources of raw materials and energy, such as coalfields and ore fields
• on the coast where it is cheap to import raw materials by sea

Heavy industry is declining in *MEDCs*. The opposite is *light industry*, which is expanding in MEDCs.

■ *e.g.* steel, shipbuilding, chemicals and oil refining.

HEP: see *hydroelectric power.*

hierarchy: placement of items in order of size and importance.

■ There are large numbers of items at the bottom of a hierarchy and only a few near the top, creating a pyramid shape. A hierarchy of settlement consists of *hamlet, village*, small town (e.g. *market town*), large town (e.g. industrial town), city and *capital city*. There are large numbers of hamlets, fewer villages, even fewer market towns, and so on until there is only one capital city. Note that as the number of settlements goes down, the number of people living there goes up, from under 100 people in a hamlet to over 1 million in many cities. The settlements also increase in importance — cities contain many more services and have a larger *sphere of influence* than market towns.

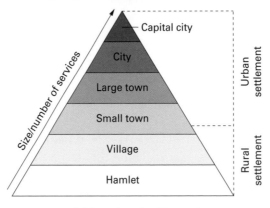

A hierarchy of settlements

A hierarchy of shops consists of corner shop, shopping parade, small town centre, city centre and capital.

high-order: describes goods and services which are expensive and purchased less often.

■ Facilities for purchasing high-order goods are found only in larger settlements. The *central business districts* of towns and cities are high-order shopping and service centres, as these offer the greatest choice and range of goods and services. Furniture is an example of a high-order good, because people only buy new furniture occasionally. A furniture shop needs to be accessible to a large population before it can be profitable.

high pressure: atmospheric condition where air sinks and the weight of air at the surface increases.

■ An area of high pressure is known as an *anticyclone.*

high-tech industry: modern industry associated with advanced technology.

■ High-tech industries make products such as computers, microelectronics, telecommunications equipment and mobile phones. Many are *footloose industries,* because the components used are small and easy to assemble at the factory. They rely on research and development to make new inventions and improvements, so highly skilled workers are essential. For this reason they are often located close to universities and on *science parks*. They also tend to be close to motorways to receive components and distribute products to markets, and are usually in pleasant locations such as *greenfield sites*.

high-yielding variety: kind of crop grown from seed developed to increase crop production.

■ High-yielding varieties were first developed in the 1960s. The *green revolution* in *LEDCs* has been based upon using these seeds.

■ *e.g.* IR-8 is a rice seed which gives up to five times more rice per hectare in India than traditionally used seeds.

honeypot: place which attracts a great numbers of visitors, especially at weekends and during school holidays.

■ Most *National Parks* have one or more areas of great visitor pressure. Honeypots experience problems, such as traffic congestion, lack of parking, litter, footpath erosion and other damage to the environment.

■ *e.g.* Honeypot sites are found in many types of location: around lakes, e.g. Windermere and Coniston Water in the Lake District; in areas of *karst* scenery, e.g. Malham and Ingleton in the Yorkshire Dales; on the coast, e.g. Lulworth Cove in Dorset. There are also examples close to large urban areas, such as Box Hill on the chalk escarpment in Surrey.

Hoyt model: model used to divide urban areas into *land use* zones.

■ The zones of the Hoyt model are arranged in sectors leading out from the *central business district* in the middle.

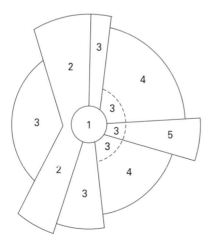

1 Central business district (CBD)
2 Wholesale light manufacturing
3 Low-class (older) residential
4 Medium-class (newer) residential
5 High-class residential

humidity: amount of water vapour in the air.
- Air is saturated when its relative humidity is 100%.

hurricane: tropical storm caused by very *low pressure*.
- Hurricanes bring very strong winds and heavy rain. They form over hot sea surfaces (above 27°C), usually in late summer and autumn when the sea surface is hottest. Energy to drive the system comes from the continuous supplies of heat and moisture. Hot air rises in strong *convection currents*. This gives very low pressure and strong winds at the surface and creates tall cumulonimbus clouds from which heavy rain falls. Hurricanes affect the Caribbean, Gulf of Mexico and neighbouring coastal areas such as Florida. In Asia, hurricanes are known as 'cyclones'. In the Far East the name 'typhoon' is also used.

Places likely to be badly affected by hurricanes
- coastal areas — the winds are strongest here and huge waves are whipped up
- *LEDCs* — people may not have advance warning of the hurricane and cannot move out of the way
- densely populated towns

Places less likely to be badly affected by hurricanes
- inland areas — hurricanes lose strength as they move inland
- *MEDCs* — television and radio channels give plenty of notice of the storm and its possible track

hydraulic action: wearing away of the Earth's surface by the force of moving water.
- Hydraulic action is a process of *erosion*. In river channels, water washes against the bed and sides, eroding them away with time. Erosion is greatest when the river is in flood. On the coastline, waves wash against and erode the bottom of cliffs, especially if the waves are *destructive waves*.

hydroelectric power (HEP): generating electricity by the force of moving water.
- Hydroelectric power requires fast-flowing rivers containing a lot of water. These are found mainly in mountainous areas, which have high *precipitation* throughout the year. A *dam* is often built to hold back water and increase the amount of electricity that can be produced. HEP is a form of *alternative energy* generated from a *renewable resource*. Its production does not pollute the atmosphere. However, if a dam is built, people may need to be moved and wildlife habitats are lost.
- *e.g.* Aswan High Dam on the River Nile in Egypt.

hydrological cycle (also called 'water cycle'): movement of water through various environments from the atmosphere and back into it.

■ A number of processes are involved in this cycle, which operates between air, land and sea. Some are shown on the sketch below.

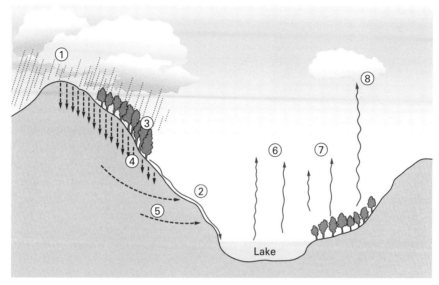

① *Precipitation*	③ *Interception*	⑤ *Groundwater flow*	⑦ *Evapotranspiration*
② *Runoff*	④ *Infiltration*	⑥ *Evaporation*	⑧ *Condensation*

ice age: period when *glaciers* grow and spread to cover areas not usually under ice.
■ At times during the last ice age the British Isles was covered by ice, except for areas south of a line from London to Bristol. There were many valley glaciers in mountainous areas, such as the Highlands of Scotland, Lake District and Snowdonia. The last ice age ended about 10,000 years ago.

ice sheet: slowly moving mass of ice covering a wide surface area.
■ *e.g.* The two largest ice sheets in the world are in Antarctica and Greenland.

igneous rock: rock formed by volcanic activity.
■ The word 'igneous' comes from the Latin word for fire. Igneous rocks are formed from *magma* which rises up from the interior of the Earth. The magma is emitted in volcanic eruptions and cools on the surface as rock.
■ *e.g.* basalt and granite.

immigration: movement of people into a country from another country.
■ Immigration is international *migration*. Some immigration is voluntary. For example, the most common *pull factor* is to find a job or better paid work. Some immigration is forced. People may be forced to move by *push factors,* such as war, changes in government, or *natural hazards* like drought and floods.

impermeable rock: rock which does not allow water to pass through it.
■ In some impermeable rocks, such as granite, there are few spaces in the rock to hold water. In others, such as clay, water seeps into the rock, where it is retained.

import: purchase of goods and services from other countries.
■ Some *trade* is essential for all countries. Few countries have all the foodstuffs, raw materials and manufactured goods they need. *MEDCs* typically import raw materials and food from *LEDCs* and some manufactured goods from *newly industrialising countries* in Asia. LEDCs typically import manufactured goods.

industrial estate: area laid out for factories.

▧ An industrial estate is normally located on the edge of a settlement, near to a main road. Factory units are built and equipped with services, such as electricity and water. Most of these factories are for *light industries*. Sometimes estates are built to attract new industries into an area. The more modern name for industrial estate is *business park*, because many are no longer just for factories but also include offices and warehouses.

industrial inertia: when an industry stays in a location even after the advantages for locating there have ceased to exist.

▧ Industrial inertia applies most to *heavy industries*. Local *raw materials* run out, but the cost of moving a big factory is too great, so the industry stays.

▧ *e.g.* steel works in Scunthorpe.

industrialisation: growth and increasing importance of *manufacturing industry*.

▧ At present, industrialisation is mainly a feature of *newly industrialising countries*. Expanding industry is helping some *LEDCs* to develop economically and improve the living standards of their people.

infant mortality rate: number of deaths of children under 1 year old per 1,000 people.

▧ Babies need clean water, good food and medical care to survive. These are not always available in *LEDCs*. The fewer infant deaths there are per 1,000 people, the better developed and richer the country. Some examples of infant mortality rates in 2000 are given below.

MEDCs		LEDCs	
Average	13 per 1,000	**Average**	60 per 1,000
UK	9 per 1,000	**Worst**	Sierra Leone in Africa estimated 200 per 1,000

infiltration: downward movement of water into soil.

▧ Infiltration is one of the processes in the *hydrological cycle*.

infrastructure: network of services needed for industries and businesses to operate successfully.

▧ Infrastructure includes:
● transport and communications (roads, railways and telephones)
● energy supply (electricity and gas)
● water and sewerage
● health and education facilities

Infrastructure is usually well supplied in *MEDCs* but lacking in many *LEDCs*, which holds back economic growth.

in-migration: movement of people into an area from another area within the same country.
■ This is a type of national *migration*. In many countries, particularly *LEDCs*, the main pattern of in-migration is into urban areas from the countryside (rural–urban migration). In *MEDCs* some people are moving into the countryside from the cities (urban–rural migration).

inner city: urban zone around the edges of the *central business district*.
■ The inner city is often associated with *urban decay*. It may feature old houses, factories and warehouses, and areas of waste ground. In some inner cities, tower blocks of flats have been built to replace houses that were removed for *slum* clearance. Better-off people have moved to the *suburbs*. Inner cities have many problems:
● environmental — wasteland, derelict buildings, unsightly tower blocks
● economic — businesses closing or relocating to the edges of the city, high unemployment rates, high levels of poverty
● social — broken families, crime, racial tension
In some areas, there has been inner-city redevelopment (see *urban redevelopment* and *gentrification*). Larger areas that have been redeveloped are often around old docks.

exam watch

Below is a brief **case study** on the redevelopment of the London Docklands.

What was the problem?
Docks had closed, warehouses and dock basins were no longer needed, local residents lost their main source of work.

In what ways has the area been redeveloped?
Warehouses have been converted into luxury flats. Spare land is used for offices, such as Canary Wharf. Transport links have been improved, e.g. by the Docklands Light Railway.

input: factor that goes into a system.
■ Inputs into a *factory system* include *raw materials*, *energy*, *capital* and *labour*. Inputs into a *farm system* include capital, seeds, *fertilisers* and pesticides.

insolation: amount of *solar* energy reaching the Earth's surface as heat.
■ Insolation is greatest in the tropics where the sun is at a higher angle in the sky. The sun's rays have a smaller area of the surface to heat up.

intensive farming: type of agriculture producing a high output per hectare from a small area of land.
■ High *inputs* into the *farm system* lead to high *outputs*. The farmer produces as much as possible from the land. To do this, a lot of *capital* is invested in seeds and *fertilisers* for crops, and in fodder for animals. In *MEDCs* many farmers

behave like businesspeople. They are said to be in *agribusiness*, using scientific methods of farming and large amounts of machinery.

■ *e.g. Market gardening* in MEDCs produces high yields of vegetables from high inputs of labour, fertiliser and water. Rice-growing in the monsoon lands of Asia is based on high inputs of labour. Two or three crops a year may be taken from each small plot of land.

interception: prevention of rain from falling directly onto the ground by trees and plants.

■ Interception is one of the processes in the *hydrological cycle*. It helps to slow down *runoff* and reduces the risk of river floods.

interdependence: describes the relationship between two or more countries with a shared need to exchange one another's goods or services.

■ Interdependence should be to the advantage of both countries. The basic pattern of world *trade* is that *LEDCs* export raw materials to be used by manufacturing industries in *MEDCs*. MEDCs export manufactured goods, many of which LEDCs cannot make for themselves. This makes LEDCs and MEDCs dependent upon one other. The major problem with this pattern of trade is that manufactured goods are of higher value than raw materials. This favours MEDCs, which become rich, while the LEDCs remain poor.

■ *e.g. Multinational companies* based in Europe benefit from setting up factories and assembling goods in the Far East, where labour rates are much lower. The countries in the Far East benefit from the jobs created and the introduction of new technology. However, the companies in Europe control what is happening and can choose to leave the Far East at any time.

interlocking spurs: ridges of overlapping higher ground in the upper course of a river valley.

■ Interlocking spurs are landforms of river *erosion*. They are formed by a river cutting vertically down into the land. Ridges stick out on alternate sides of the valley. The river winds (but does not *meander*) from side to side around the ridges.

intermediate technology: see *appropriate technology*.

invisible trade: international trade in services.

■ Although this trade can be measured in money, no goods are exchanged. Invisible trade includes:

● tourism — visitors spend money on accommodation, food, transport and entertainment
● banking and insurance — for allowing international business
● shipping and aircraft — for moving people and goods around the world
● telecommunications — keeping in touch worldwide by phone, fax and e-mail
● workers — people earning money by working overseas

irrigation: artificially adding water to farm land.

Irrigation takes place where rainfall is insufficient or too unreliable for crop growing. Irrigation water is often stored behind a *dam*. Water is distributed in the fields either in channels between rows of crops or by overhead sprinklers.

e.g. In *deserts*, crop-growing is impossible without the use of irrigation water, as in the Nile valley in Egypt (part of the Sahara Desert). Irrigation can also be used in wetter regions to increase crop yields. For example, potato farmers in East Anglia often irrigate to make their potatoes grow bigger.

joint: vertical crack within a layer of rock.

▓ A joint is a line of weakness in the rock which allows *weathering* and *erosion* to take place. *Carboniferous limestone* has both joints and *bedding planes,* which helps to explain why it forms *karst* scenery.

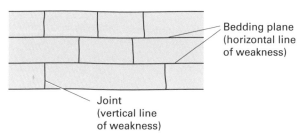

Layers of sedimentary rock

Bedding plane (horizontal line of weakness)

Joint (vertical line of weakness)

karst: landforms and landscapes which occur in areas of *Carboniferous limestone*.

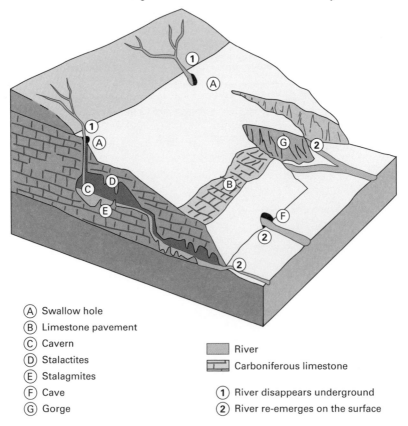

(A) Swallow hole
(B) Limestone pavement
(C) Cavern
(D) Stalactites
(E) Stalagmites
(F) Cave
(G) Gorge

River
Carboniferous limestone

(1) River disappears underground
(2) River re-emerges on the surface

■ Karst scenery has both surface and underground features. Surface landforms include *swallow holes*, limestone pavements and *gorges*. Underground features include *caves, caverns, stalactites and stalagmites*. The features are formed by limestone *solution*, which widens *joints* and *bedding planes*.

■ *e.g.* Yorkshire Dales.

labour: work done by people.

■ Labour is an *input* into *factory systems* and *farm systems*. An appropriate labour supply is very important. For example, high-tech industries require skilled workers. In *MEDCs* the amount of labour needed has been reduced by the use of machines and robots. In *LEDCs* many factories and farms are labour intensive, which means they rely upon people more than machines. Wage rates in LEDCs are lower than in MEDCs.

landfill site: large hole in the ground, such as an old quarry, into which waste is dumped.

landform: physical feature of the Earth's surface with a distinctive shape.

■ Landforms are created by *erosion, deposition* and *weathering*. The table below gives some examples.

River erosion	V-shaped valley, interlocking spurs, waterfall, gorge, river cliff
River deposition	slip-off slope, levée, floodplain, delta
Glacial erosion	corrie, U-shaped valley, hanging valley, ribbon lake
Glacial deposition	moraine (e.g. terminal moraine), drumlin
Coastal erosion	cliff, wave-cut platform, cave, arch, stack, headland, bay
Coastal deposition	beach, spit, bar, tombolo

land use: the way the Earth's surface is used.

■ Land uses in rural areas include crops, grass, woodland, moorland and marsh. In urban areas they include houses, factories, offices, shops and open spaces.

latitude: lines running parallel to the equator.

■ The base line is the *equator* (0°). There are 90° of latitude north and south of this line. The Tropic of Cancer is at 23.5°N, the Tropic of Capricorn is at 23.5°S, the Arctic Circle is at 66.5°N and the Antarctic Circle is at 66.5°S. The UK lies between 50°N and 60°N. The location of any place can be fixed by knowing its latitude and *longitude*.

lava: name given to *magma* after it has flowed out of a *volcano*.

■ After a volcanic eruption, lava cools and builds up to form volcanic cones and plateaux. At a *constructive plate boundary, basic lava* pours out from underground. Basic lava flows for long distances before cooling, and forms *shield volcanoes* with wide bases and gentle sides. At a *destructive plate boundary, acid lava* is released from vents. Acid lava flows only short distances before cooling, and forms cones that are narrow and steep sided.

leaching: downward movement of minerals through soil, caused by water transportation.

■ Leaching makes the soil less fertile because minerals are taken out of reach of plant roots. It takes place in those areas where *precipitation* is greater than *evaporation*. One example of a leached soil is *podsol*.

LEDC (less economically developed country): poor country with a low level of development.

■ LEDCs are located to the south of the dividing line between North and South (see *development*). People living in LEDCs are less wealthy and have a lower quality of life than those living in more economically developed countries (*MEDCs*) to the north of the line. Different indicators show that these countries are less economically developed. Some examples are given below.

Indicator	Average for all LEDCs	Average for all MEDCs
Gross domestic product (US$ per head)	3,000	16,000
Employment (% in agriculture)	58	8
Life expectancy (years at birth)	62	75
Access to safe water (% of the population)	71	100
Literacy rate (% of adults who can read and write)	65	100

leeward: describes an area sheltered from the direction in which the wind is blowing.

■ The UK's *prevailing winds* are westerly, therefore the leeward side is to the east of high ground, such as on the eastern side of the Pennines.

less economically developed country: see *LEDC*.

levée: raised bank along the side of a river, built of *silt* from river floods.

■ A levée is a landform of river *deposition*. Every time the river leaves its channel and floods, a new layer of silt is left on the bank. This builds up into a high bank over time. Natural levées are often strengthened by people and made into embankments to try to prevent flooding. This is an example of river *management*.

life expectancy: average number of years a new-born baby is expected to live.
- Life expectancy has increased everywhere in the world largely due to improvements in medical treatment, although it is still higher in *MEDCs* than in *LEDCs*. As life expectancy has gone up, *death rates* have gone down. However, in some African countries, after years of increasing, life expectancy is now beginning to drop again due to HIV and AIDS.

light industry: industry making goods using fewer bulky *raw materials* and less *energy* than *heavy industry.*
- Light industries are *footloose industries,* with considerable freedom of location. Many assemble components and need to locate near to good road transport. Light industries are widely distributed throughout the UK. Many towns have some light industries situated on *industrial estates*. However, one of the greatest concentrations of these industries is in and around London and along the M4 corridor. Proximity to the large and wealthy market of London and the southeast is a great advantage.
- *e.g.* industries making food and drink, clothing and electrical goods.

linear: describes the layout of a long, thin settlement.
- Many settlements, especially villages, are linear because they have grown by following the sides of main roads (see *ribbon development*).

literacy rate: percentage of adults who are able to read and write.
- The literacy rate is used as an indicator of a country's level of *development*. In *MEDCs*, so few adults are illiterate that the rate is usually given as 100%. In *LEDCs* there are great variations from country to country. In many African countries the literacy rate is under 50%. The rate also varies greatly between different parts of one country. For example, in rural areas in LEDCs the percentage who can read and write is lower than in the towns. There may also be differences between social groups. For example, there may be many more boys attending school than girls.

load: material transported by rivers, glaciers and the sea.
- A river's load often changes from boulders in its upper course to *silt* in its lower course. A river can carry more sediment when in flood, which is why its colour turns brown at these times.

  The load carried by the sea depends upon the type of material that is available. Along some stretches of coast, waves carry sand, whereas along others they carry shingle.

  Glaciers are so thick and large that they can carry bigger boulders than rivers and the sea. An *erratic* is a large boulder deposited within an area covered by *boulder clay.*

longitude: lines which join the north and south poles.
- The base line is the Greenwich meridian (0°), which is used to define the

world's time zones. Unlike lines of *latitude*, lines of longitude do not run parallel to each other. Instead, they meet at the poles and are widest apart at the equator. The location of any place can be fixed by knowing its latitude and longitude.

long profile: summary of the shape and gradient of a river bed, from source to *mouth*.

■ A typical river long profile can be split into upper, middle and lower courses.

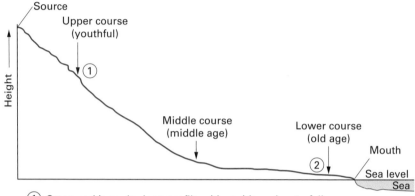

① Steep and irregular long profile with rapids and waterfalls

② Gentle and smooth long profile

longshore drift: movement of sediment along a coastline, caused by wave transportation.

■ When a wave breaks along a coastline at an angle, it also pushes pebbles up the beach at an angle. However, the *backwash* is always at right angles to the coastline. Pebbles roll back down the beach at right angles before being picked up by another wave and moved further along the coast.

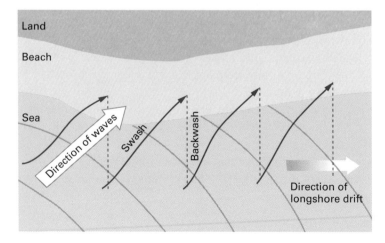

Winds determine the direction of longshore drift along a coast. Along the UK coast of the English Channel it is from west to east, driven by *prevailing winds* from the west. Down the east coast of the UK it is from north to south, because in the North Sea the dominant winds blow from the north.

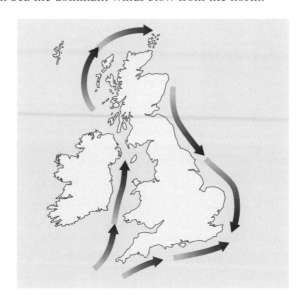

low-order: describes goods and services which are cheap and purchased regularly.

▨ Low-order goods are low value and bought often, sometimes daily. They are sold by corner shops and other local shops that have small *spheres of influence*. Most are *convenience goods*.

▨ *e.g.* newspapers, milk and chocolate.

low pressure: atmospheric condition where air rises and the weight of air at the surface becomes lower than average.

▨ In the UK, an area of low pressure forms a *depression*. In the tropics, areas of very low pressure can form *hurricanes*. When air rises, creating low pressure, cloud and rain usually result.

magma: molten rock inside the Earth.

▨ Magma is erupted onto the Earth's surface by *volcanoes* at *plate* boundaries. On the surface it cools as *lava* and builds up a volcanic cone.

malnutrition: lack of adequate nutrition caused by shortage of food or an unbalanced diet.

▨ People suffering from malnutrition become unhealthy and are less able to fight off disease. The condition is especially serious for babies and can lead to high rates of *infant mortality*.

management: controlling development and change, planning ahead.

▨ Management can be used to ensure that developments are *sustainable* or to balance the interests of different people to stop conflicts arising.

River management — rivers are very useful and so people attempt to manage them for their own purposes. In addition, a lot of people live close to rivers, and management is used to reduce the risk of floods. Examples of river management include:

● building *dams* and *reservoirs*
● increasing the height of *levées* with embankments
● building walls to control the course of the channel in urban areas

Coastal management — sometimes *groynes* are built to encourage the accumulation of beach materials in seaside resorts. In other places, sea walls, *groynes* and *gabions* are used for *coastal protection*.

manufacturing industry: industry which transforms *raw materials* or components into other products, usually in a *factory*.

▨ *Energy* and *labour* are needed to change raw materials into finished products. In a *heavy industry*, such as a steel works, large amounts of raw materials and energy are used. In a *light industry*, such as a car factory, parts are bought in and assembled along a production line. Manufacturing industry is declining in some *MEDCs* but expanding in some *LEDCs*, especially those described as *newly industrialising countries*. Manufacturing is also known as *secondary industry*.

market: place where goods and services are sold.

▦ Market accessibility is a factor taken into account by nearly all companies when choosing a new location. The largest market in the UK, with the greatest concentration of wealthy people, is London and the southeast. Being close to the market is most attractive to *light industries*, which make the finished goods that consumers buy. Markets are much smaller in many *LEDCs* where people are poorer and have little money to spend on buying goods. The only exception is in the big cities where the majority of wealthy people live. Lack of a market discourages new industries from setting up.

market gardening: type of *intensive farming* specialising in vegetables, fruit and flowers.

▦ Farms are small, but a lot of time and money is invested in them. *Inputs* are great but so are *outputs*. Market gardening is often carried out around the edges of towns and cities so that the produce can reach the urban market fresh.

Below is a brief **case study** on market gardening in the Netherlands.

In Holland, market gardening takes place on polders around and between main cities, such as Amsterdam and The Hague. The farms grow salad vegetables (lettuces, tomatoes and cucumbers), soft fruits (such as strawberries) and flowers.

Why is market gardening important in this area?
- fertile soils on land reclaimed from the sea
- sand and silt soils which warm up quickly and are easy to work
- large local market in the cities
- easy to export to other EU countries by road and to the UK by sea

Why is it an example of intensive farming?
- inputs are high — labour, fertilisers and heating in the greenhouses
- outputs are high — two or three crops are grown on the same piece of land each year

market town: relatively small *rural settlement* which serves people living in the surrounding area.

▦ Market towns have a variety of shops and other services, such as banks and solicitors. Most continue to hold a market on one day each week as they have done for centuries. The population is between 5,000 and 20,000. Some have grown in recent years as living in the countryside becomes more popular. They may have an *industrial estate*, but they are rarely industrial towns.

▦ *e.g.* Richmond in North Yorkshire serves Swaledale.

meander: bend in a river, usually along its middle or lower course.

▦ Once the river begins to flow against the outside bend of a meander, the force

exam watch

of the flowing water is concentrated there. Lateral *erosion* leads to the formation of a *river cliff* and causes the meander to widen. On the inside bend, where the flow is slower, a more gentle *slip-off slope* is formed by *deposition*.

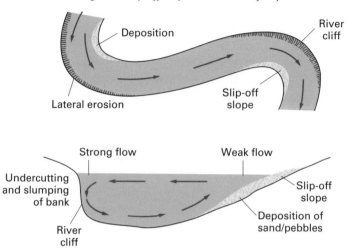

mechanical weathering: see *physical weathering.*

MEDC (more economically developed country): wealthy country with a high level of development.

▨ MEDCs are located to the north of the dividing line between North and South (see *development*). They are richer, and in some cases considerably richer, than the *LEDCs* to the south of the line. Most are in North America and Europe, but they include Japan, Australia and New Zealand. Some characteristics of MEDCs are given below.

Gross domestic product	High (average of US$16,000 per head)
Employment	High percentage employed in services (average 60%)
Life expectancy	High (average of 75 years)
Natural increase of population	Low (below 0.5%)

mega-city: very large city with over 10 million inhabitants.

▨ Asia has more mega-cities than any other continent. China and India have most because of their large populations and continuing rural–urban *migration*.

▨ *e.g.* Tokyo and Beijing.

metamorphic rock: rock altered by heat and pressure.

▨ *e.g.* Limestone (a *sedimentary rock*) can be altered by heat and pressure to become marble (a metamorphic rock). Marble is harder than limestone and can be used for building. Slate is a metamorphic rock, formed from clay, which can be used for roofing.

mid-ocean ridge: mountain range on the ocean floor along a *constructive plate boundary*.

■ A mid-ocean ridge is formed by *magma* from the interior of the Earth flowing out as runny *basic lava* and cooling as basalt, a type of *igneous rock*.

■ *e.g.* the mid-Atlantic ridge. Some of the volcanoes in this ridge appear above the ocean surface as volcanic islands. The island of Surtsey, off the south coast of Iceland, was created in 1963.

migration: movement of people to live in a different place.

■ People move due to *push factors*, or *pull factors*, or a mixture of the two. Migration can be classified in different ways:

● **Forced migration** — people are driven out. This may be because of *natural hazards,* such as *floods, droughts, earthquakes* and *volcanoes,* or human problems, such as wars, changes in government and crime.

● **Voluntary migration** — people choose to move. This may be to find work or a better paid job, or to have better services (health, education, electricity and sanitation).

● **National migration** — people move within a country. In *LEDCs* the greatest movement is rural–urban (from the countryside into the cities). In *MEDCs* some movement is urban–rural (from the city into the surrounding rural areas).

● **International migration** — people move to another country. Sometimes men migrate to work in another country, and their families may join them later. In some places, wars and hazards create *refugees* as people are forced to flee.

millionaire city: large city with more than 1 million inhabitants.

■ There are at least 300 millionaire cities in the world, mostly in Asia, Europe and North America. There are an increasing number of millionaire cities in *LEDCs*. This is due to rapid *urbanisation* caused by:

● continued rural–urban *migration*

● high rates of *natural increase* in population

mining: removal of minerals from the ground.

■ Minerals are *non-renewable resources,* such as coal, oil, copper and iron ore.

mixed farming: type of agriculture based on keeping animals and growing crops together on one farm.

■ Most farms in the UK used to be of this type. Animals manured the fields and fertilised the land for crops to be grown. Crops were fed to the animals in winter. Today, farmers are more likely to specialise in either crops or livestock.

monoculture: cultivation of just one crop.

■ *Plantations* in the tropics produce a single crop, such as coffee or bananas. The same happens in vineyards and apple orchards in temperate regions. Monoculture mainly involves trees or bush crops which continue to produce

for many years. Problems associated with monoculture include:
- income goes down when prices fall
- pests and diseases can spread through the whole crop and wipe it out
- sprays and fertilisers are needed to maintain output

monsoon: season of heavy rainfall in countries such as India.

■ In monsoon climates, there is a wet season in summer and it is dry for the rest of the year. In summer, winds blow off the sea and bring rain. The heavy rains are used by rice farmers in India. If the rains fail to arrive, yields of rice are lower and many people suffer from *malnutrition*.

moraine: collective term for all transported materials dropped by a *glacier* when it melts.

■ Moraine is a product of glacial *deposition*. It is made up of an unsorted mixture of clay and boulders of different sizes, called *boulder clay*. There are four types of moraine:
- lateral moraine — line down the sides of a valley
- medial moraine — line down the middle of a valley
- *terminal moraine* — line across the end of a valley
- ground moraine — spread everywhere across the land as undulating areas of boulder clay

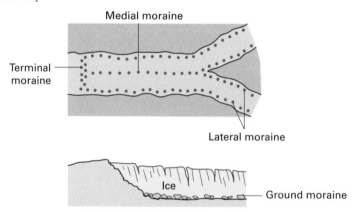

more economically developed country: see *MEDC*.

morphology: shape and structure of an item.

■ Urban morphology is the shape and structure of a city. The *Burgess model* attempts to show the urban zones that can be recognised in many urban areas.

mouth: point at which a river enters the sea.

■ If the river enters the sea by only one channel, the mouth is an *estuary*. If it enters by many separate channels (or *distributaries*), the mouth is a *delta*.

multicultural: describes a country or area which is home to people from different ethnic, racial and religious backgrounds.

■ The UK is a multicultural country. Since the 1950s, significant numbers of *immigrants* have arrived from Asia and the West Indies, as well as some from Africa and Eastern Europe. These people have brought many languages and different religions and customs to the UK. Inner city areas of large cities, such as London and Birmingham, have large multicultural populations. Leicester is the first city in the UK to have more than half its population of Asian origin.

The USA is an even clearer example of a multicultural society. The population is almost entirely made up of immigrants from almost every country in the world. In recent years, the greatest number of immigrants to the USA have come from Spanish-speaking Mexico, Central American countries and Caribbean islands.

multinational company (also called 'transnational corporation'): large business with interests in many countries.

■ Multinationals usually have headquarters located in *MEDCs*, especially in the USA, European Union and Japan. Business operations are present in both MEDCs and *LEDCs*, but workers have little influence over the decisions taken in company headquarters. This is an example of how *globalisation* works. Multinational companies are involved in many different economic activities, as shown below.

Economic activities	Multinational companies
Food and drink	McDonald's, Coca-Cola, Cadbury-Schweppes
Cars	Ford, General Motors, Toyota
Computing and electronics	IBM, Siemens, Fujitsu
Oil	Shell, Exxon, BP-Amoco

multiplier effect: concept stating that once one successful business grows in an area, other businesses will benefit and expand as well.

■ The multiplier effect can start a cycle of growth like the one shown below. It is the reason why governments and local councils welcome new investments from big companies.

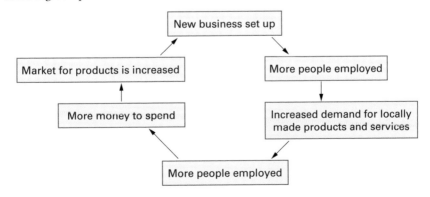

National Park: area of natural beauty and relatively wild countryside managed by government.

■ A National Park needs *management* to:

● preserve its natural beauty

● provide facilities for visitors

Within a National Park, restrictions are put on building new houses, roads and factories to stop the loss of countryside. Car parks, picnic sites and footpaths are planned so that visitors have access but in a controlled way.

■ *e.g.* The world's first National Park was Yellowstone in the USA. Kenya has parks in which big game animals are protected against hunters for visitors to view on safari. There are 11 National Parks in England and Wales, the majority in the upland areas of the north and west.

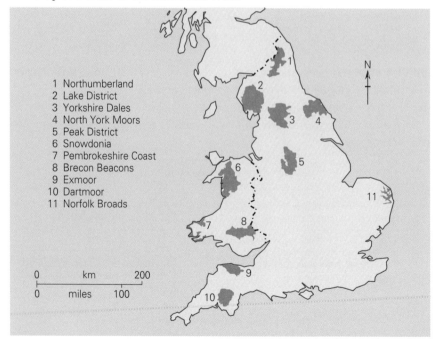

1 Northumberland
2 Lake District
3 Yorkshire Dales
4 North York Moors
5 Peak District
6 Snowdonia
7 Pembrokeshire Coast
8 Brecon Beacons
9 Exmoor
10 Dartmoor
11 Norfolk Broads

Below is a brief **case study** of conflicts in a National Park.

Large numbers of visitors cause:
- pressure around the most popular *honeypot* sites
- footpath erosion along the most popular paths

Conflicts develop between:
- visitors and farmers
- visitors and local residents
- different groups of visitors with varied interests

Visitors may aggravate farmers by:
- leaving gates open
- dropping litter
- walking through fields of crops
- climbing over and damaging dry stone walls
- having dogs off the lead which worry sheep

natural decrease: population decrease because the *death rate* is higher than the *birth rate*, i.e. the number of deaths in a year is greater than the number of live births.

■ Natural decrease is happening in some European countries where birth rates have fallen to very low levels. Natural decrease leads to an increased percentage of elderly people (see *ageing population*).

■ *e.g.* The table below shows two examples of natural decrease in 1999.

Country	Birth rate per 1,000	Death rate per 1,000	Natural decrease per 1,000
Italy	9.1	9.9	0.8 (0.08%)
Germany	9.3	10.3	1.0 (0.1%)

natural gas: *fossil fuel* found in underground traps, often close to where oil is present.

■ Natural gas is a source of *energy*. Its use and importance is increasing because it emits less pollution into the atmosphere than it burns than coal and oil. In the UK there has been a 'dash for gas' as power stations have turned to using natural gas instead of coal for making electricity. However, natural gas is a *non-renewable resource*.

■ *e.g.* The UK has its own natural gas fields in the North Sea and Morecambe Bay.

natural hazard: short-term event that is a threat to life and property.

■ Natural hazards are caused by natural events, such as *earthquakes, volcanoes* and *hurricanes*. These events are unpredictable, and people and property are never safe while they are happening. Earthquakes are the most unpredictable.

No one can tell when they are going to happen. Sometimes there are warning signs that a volcano is about to erupt, but these are also unpredictable. The formation and movement of hurricanes can be followed by satellite, but they can change track at any time.

Loss of life from natural hazards is often greater in *LEDCs*, because governments and people cannot afford to prepare for them. People are also less likely to be given or to hear warnings of the arrival of hurricanes. The value of property lost may be greater in *MEDCs* because buildings and possessions are worth more. However, people in MEDCs are more likely to have insurance. Again, this means that rich people suffer less from natural hazards than poor people.

Primary (direct) effects of a natural hazard
Buildings are destroyed and people killed.

Secondary effects of a natural hazard
These follow from the primary effects, e.g. shortage of food and spread of disease.

natural increase: population growth because the *birth rate* is higher than the *death rate*.
- The size of a country's natural increase is calculated in the following way:
    birth rate – death rate = rate of natural increase
The average rate of natural increase (per 1,000) in *MEDCs* is: 13 – 10 = 3. Natural increase is often stated as the number per 100 (i.e. as a percentage). This gives an average rate of increase of 0.3% per year in MEDCs. The average rate of increase (per 1,000) in *LEDCs* is: 27 – 9 = 16 (or 1.6% per year).

High rates of natural increase (over 25 per 1,000, or 2.5%) are found in countries where birth rates remain high while death rates fall. The majority of these countries are in Africa and are mainly in stage 2 of the *demographic transition model*.

natural resource: naturally occurring material which can be used by people.
- Some natural resources are used as food, but many are used as *raw materials* in industries.
- *e.g.* forests on the land surface, minerals underground, fish in the sea.

natural vegetation: trees and plants which grow if land is untouched by people.
- The most important factor determining the natural vegetation of a place is *climate*. This is why natural vegetation is also called 'climatic climax vegetation'. *Tropical rainforest* is the natural vegetation of places with a hot and wet climate near the equator. Before people cleared the land for farming and settlement, the natural vegetation cover over most of the British Isles was deciduous woodland.

neighbourhood: local residential area in towns and cities.

■ In a neighbourhood, services are provided for the use of residents within easy walking distance, such as shops selling *convenience goods*, a primary school and public house. In British *New Towns*, residential neighbourhood units with their own services were part of the original town plan. One aim was to try to give people a sense of belonging to the area where they lived. Another was to keep out through traffic.

newly industrialising countries: see *NIC*.

New Town: planned settlement built over a short period of time.

■ Most towns grow naturally over a long period of time. By contrast, New Towns are built rapidly when planners decide more houses are needed. The earliest New Towns in the UK were built beyond the *green belt* on *greenfield sites* around large urban areas. For example, a ring of eight New Towns was built around London. People and businesses from London moved into the New Towns to reduce overcrowding and congestion in London.

■ *e.g.* Milton Keynes is the UK's largest New Town. It is located further away from London than the earlier New Towns, but is well placed for transport near to the M1. It could be described as a new city, as it has a large central shopping centre and a wide range of facilities for leisure and recreation.

NIC (newly industrialising country): *LEDC* which is experiencing rapid growth in *secondary industry*.

■ In NICs, the percentage of the workforce employed in secondary industry is increasing. The countries are developing economically. Factors encouraging growth of secondary industries include:
● cheap wage rates
● plentiful labour supply
● growing home markets
● government support
● investment by multinational companies
● easy export
  Multinational companies build factories in these countries because costs of production are so much lower than in *MEDCs*. Some of the older examples of NICs, especially Singapore and Hong Kong, have developed so much that they now have many of the characteristics associated with MEDCs.

■ *e.g.* Brazil and Mexico in Latin America; Taiwan, South Korea and Malaysia in Asia.

non-renewable resource: *natural resource* which can only be used once.

■ This category includes all the Earth's mineral resources. There is great concern about the speed at which *fossil fuels* (coal, oil and natural gas) are being used up. These provide a high proportion of world energy needs, but known reserves are limited.

exam watch

nuclear power: generating electricity by splitting the nuclei of uranium or plutonium atoms.

In the UK, about one quarter of the electricity used is generated from nuclear power. In some *MEDCs*, such as France and Japan, which do not have large *fossil fuel* resources of their own, the proportion is much higher.

Views in favour of nuclear power
- It doesn't pollute the atmosphere. It doesn't contribute to *global warming* and *acid rain*.
- A lot of energy is released using only a little uranium.
- It saves oil for better uses, such as diesel and petrol for transport.

Views against nuclear power
- It is dangerous to health. It releases radioactivity which causes cancers in people.
- There is a danger of explosion and widespread nuclear contamination, as with the Chernobyl disaster.
- Nuclear waste remains radioactive for thousands of years and there is no safe means of disposal.

occluded front: dividing line where a *cold front* joins up with a *warm front*.

■ At an occluded front, all the warm air is lifted up from the surface, producing a wide band of cloud and rain.

opencast mining: extracting minerals from the surface of the Earth.

■ The process of opencast mining is the same as *quarrying*. The topsoil is removed and minerals, such as coal, are loosened by blasting and scraped out by diggers. It leaves behind a large hole in the ground, which is either filled back in or used as a *landfill site*. Opencast mining is unpopular with local residents. It creates a lot of noise, large amounts of dust and the heavy trucks used to carry minerals away lead to road congestion. Mining companies prefer this method to underground mining. It is cheaper and easier to dig from the surface because more and bigger machinery can be used.

organic farming: type of agriculture which does not use chemical *fertilisers*, pesticides and artificial growth stimulants.

■ This is farming in a *sustainable* way.

out-migration: movement of people out of an area into another area within the same country.

■ This is a type of national *migration*. In many countries, particularly *LEDCs*, the main pattern of out-migration is out of rural areas and into urban areas (rural–urban migration). In *MEDCs*, some people are moving out of the cities into the rural areas (urban–rural migration).

out-of-town location: site on the edge of a built-up area or in the rural area beyond.

■ Out-of-town locations have become popular with supermarkets, shopping centres, factories and *business parks*. They use *greenfield sites*, which offer more space for buildings and car parks. The land is often cheaper and more can be used. Locations near to main roads and motorway junctions are the most sought after.

output: factor that is the end product of a system.

O

■ The main outputs from a *factory system* are the goods to be sold. Money from the sale of outputs is used to purchase *inputs* and pay for the processes that keep the factory running as a profitable business. There are also other less profitable outputs from a factory system, such as waste.

overgrazing: destruction of grass and other vegetation caused by too many animals on the land.

■ When overgrazing occurs, bare ground begins to show between the grasses. This ground may then be eroded by wind and rain. Increases in the amount of bare ground can lead to *desertification* in dry areas, such as in the Sahel on the southern edge of the Sahara Desert.

overpopulation: too many people in an area to be provided for by the available resources.

■ In overpopulated areas, resources are insufficient either to feed everyone or to give everyone a good standard of living. Overpopulation is more of a problem in *LEDCs* than in *MEDCs*. In LEDCs, after many years of high rates of *natural increase*, the growth of people has outpaced the resources available.

exam watch

Overpopulation is not the same as having a high population density. If an area has good resources, then it can support a lot of people without becoming over-populated.

oxbow lake: semi-circular lake on the *floodplain* of a river.

■ An oxbow lake is a landform of river *erosion*. It forms when a river cuts through the outside bend of a *meander* and flows straight. This usually happens when the river is in flood. The old meander loop is cut off and the lake is sealed by new deposits of silt.

ozone layer: area of ozone gas in the upper atmosphere.

■ Ozone is a type of oxygen which filters the sun's ultra-violet rays, so protecting the Earth from radiation damage. The thinning of the ozone layer is blamed for the increase in the number of skin cancers. A large ozone hole has been discovered over Antarctica. Each winter it increases in size and extends over a wider area. Thinning of the ozone layer has also been detected over the Arctic. Emission of chlorofluorocarbons (CFCs) from aerosol sprays and refrigeration equipment was discovered to be the main cause. Now that the use of these has been banned it is hoped that the size of the ozone hole each winter will soon begin to decrease.

exam watch

The hole in the ozone layer is not the same as the greenhouse effect and global warming. Many candidates make the mistake of writing that the hole in the ozone layer allows the sun to heat up the Earth more.

Pacific Ring of Fire: line of *volcanoes* following the *destructive plate boundaries* around the sides of the Pacific Ocean.

▨ The Pacific Ring of Fire circles the Pacific Ocean on the mainland in the Americas and through the islands of Asia and the South Pacific. It is one of the world's most active *earthquake* belts.

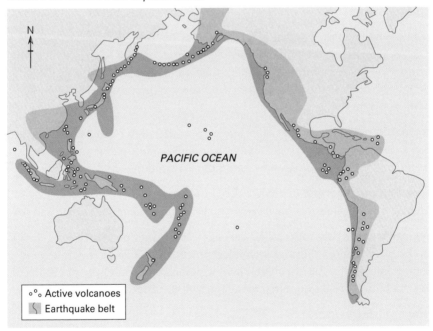

park and ride: facility providing car parking outside a city and bus transport into the city centre.

▨ This is an attempt to solve the problems of traffic congestion in city centres.

pastoral farming: type of agriculture based on keeping livestock, such as cows and sheep.

▨ There are different types of pastoral farming. In the UK there is dairy farming, beef cattle rearing, sheep farming and pig farming. These are mainly practised by farmers living in the wetter west and uplands, where grass grows better than crops. In some *LEDCs* there is a different type called *pastoral nomadism*. The opposite of pastoral farming is *arable farming*.

pastoral nomadism: type of agriculture involving farmers moving from place to place with their animals.

■ Pastoral nomads practise *subsistence farming,* living off the milk and meat of their camels, goats, sheep and cattle. This type of farming is mainly found in Africa and the Middle East, in areas with a dry climate or where there is a dry season. Farmers need to move to find new pastures for grazing. It is an example of *extensive farming* because large areas of land are needed and *inputs* and *outputs* are low. Its importance is declining as more land is needed for permanent settlement. In addition, *overgrazing* in dry areas leads to *desertification*.

pedestrianisation: closing roads to traffic for the use of people on foot.

■ It is now common in city centres for one or more roads to be closed to traffic for most of the time. The area is then reserved for the use of shoppers and visitors on foot.

periphery: area at the edge or of less economic importance.

■ The periphery is where economic activity declines. It may be a rural area with lower levels of economic development than an urban area. In some *LEDCs* the periphery refers to the entire country outside the capital city. The opposite of periphery is *core*.

permeable rock: rock with spaces and gaps so that water can pass through it.

■ *e.g. Carboniferous limestone* has many *joints* and *bedding planes* through which water, and even surface streams, can disappear underground.

physical factor: natural or environmental feature.

■ The main physical factors are *relief*, drainage, *climate, natural vegetation* and soil.

physical weathering (also called 'mechanical weathering')**:** break-up of rock in the place where it lies by mechanical processes such as *freeze–thaw*.

■ In physical weathering, the minerals which make up the rock are not changed. The rock itself breaks up, often along lines of weakness such as *joints*.

plain: level, lowland area.

■ Plains are most likely next to coasts or rivers. The flat land next to a river in its lower course is a *floodplain*, which is built up by silt deposits from river floods.

plantation: large farm in the tropics where only one *cash crop* is grown.

■ A plantation is an example of *commercial farming* on a large scale. The crop is often a bush or tree crop, such as coffee, tea, rubber or bananas. Many plantations are owned and run by *multinational companies*. The crops are grown almost entirely for export.

■ *e.g.* Del Monte has banana and pineapple plantations in the Americas.

plate: enormous piece of rock which makes up a section of the Earth's crust.

■ There are seven large plates and many smaller ones. They are moving slowly, by 1–10 cm a year. The boundaries of these plates are places of great *tectonic activity*. *Volcanoes*, *earthquakes* and *fold mountains* are formed along *destructive plate boundaries* where two plates converge and one is destroyed. Volcanoes and *mid-ocean ridges* are formed along *constructive plate boundaries* where two plates diverge.

plateau: level area of land high above sea level.

■ *e.g.* Central Brazil and Tibet.

plucking: removal of pieces of rock from the Earth's surface by a *glacier*.

■ Plucking is a process of glacial *erosion*. As a glacier moves, the ice sticks to rock surfaces and pulls pieces of rock away. This happens suddenly and leaves rock outcrops with jagged edges. Plucking is more effective on rocks with many *joints*.

plunge pool: circular area of deep water at the bottom of a *waterfall*.

■ A plunge pool is formed by:
● the force of the falling water (*hydraulic action*)
● swirling boulders eroding the rock on the river bed (*abrasion*)

podsol: type of soil common in the British Isles.

■ Podsol forms under forests of coniferous trees and in sandy areas. It is an infertile soil. Minerals are lost from the top part of the soil by the downward movement of rainwater (see *leaching*). The minerals are redeposited lower down in a hard layer known as the iron pan.

pollution: contamination of the natural environment as a result of human activities.

■ There is air, land and water pollution. Some people also include noise pollution and visual pollution. Most air pollution, such as *acid rain* and *global warming*, is caused by burning *fossil fuels*. The worst land and water pollution is caused by materials which do not break down easily, such as lead and plastics. Oil spills break up naturally after a time, but only after they have damaged natural habitats and their wildlife.

population density: number of people per square kilometre.

■ Population density is calculated by the formula:

$$\text{population density} = \frac{\text{area}}{\text{total population}}$$

Population density is shown on a map by using shading for different density values placed in classes: the heavier the shading, the greater the population density.

population distribution: pattern of people in an area.

■ Population distribution is usually shown by a dot map. One dot represents a certain number of people.

population pyramid: diagram to show the *population structure* of a country or place by age and sex.

■ A population pyramid consists of horizontal bars. Numbers or percentages of males and females are plotted on different sides of the central dividing line (see *population structure*).

population structure: make-up of the population of a country or place by age and sex.

■ Population structure is shown by a *population pyramid*. In *LEDCs* population structure is dominated by children under 15 years. This gives a population pyramid with a wide base. *Life expectancy* is low, therefore the top of the pyramid is low and narrow. In *MEDCs* there is a more even distribution between the different age groups. *Birth rates* are low, therefore the percentage of children is smaller than in LEDCs. Life expectancy is high, which makes the top of the pyramid higher and wider than in LEDCs.

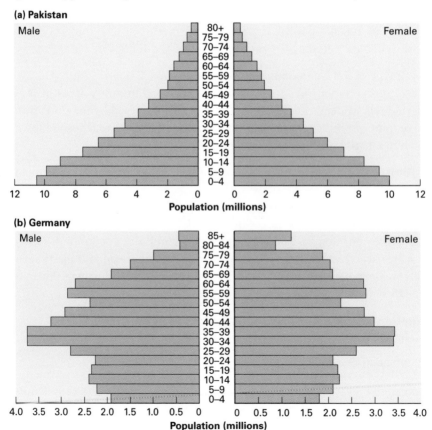

pothole: small, round hollow in the rocky bed of a river.

▥ Potholes form where hard rock outcrops on the river bed. Weaknesses in the rock are widened by stones being swirled around (see *abrasion*). Potholes are most likely to form in the river's upper course.

In general use, the word 'pothole' has another meaning. Some people go 'potholing', meaning that they are going down a *swallow hole* to explore the caverns and cave systems in *Carboniferous limestone*.

poverty cycle: vicious circle in which poor people become trapped.

▥ The poverty cycle operates among the rural poor in *LEDCs* and the urban poor in *MEDCs*.

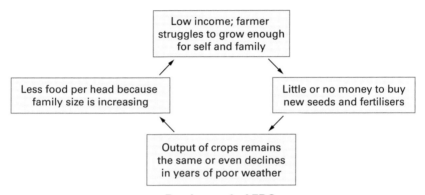

Rural areas in *LEDCs*

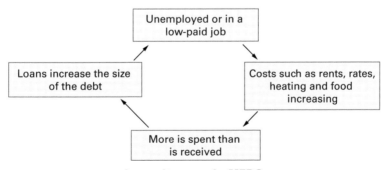

Inner city areas in *MEDCs*

power station: place where electricity is generated.

▥ The different types of power station are classified according to the source of energy used:

● thermal power — energy released from burning *fossil fuels,* mainly coal but also natural gas and oil (e.g. Ferrybridge in Yorkshire)

- *nuclear power* — energy released from splitting atoms of uranium and plutonium (e.g. Sizewell in Suffolk)
- *hydroelectric power* — energy released from the force of flowing water (e.g. Aswan High Dam in Egypt)

precipitation: all moisture that reaches the Earth's surface, irrespective of type.
Precipitation includes rain, snow and hail from the atmosphere, and fog, dew and frost on or near the ground surface. These are all caused in the same way. Moisture present in air is cooled below its *dew-point* temperature so that water vapour condenses into droplets (see *condensation*). Rain, snow and hail form after warm air has risen into the atmosphere, causing it to cool. Fog, dew and frost form after air has been cooled by contact with the cold ground surface. The formation of precipitation is one of the processes in the *hydrological cycle*.

prevailing wind: wind direction that occurs most frequently at a place.
e.g. Throughout the UK, *westerlies* are the most frequent winds.

primary industry: activity in which *raw materials* are collected but not altered in any way.
The name 'primary' is used because these were the first human activities. They remain most important in *LEDCs*, where an average 60% of the working population are farmers. As a country develops economically, the percentage working in primary industry falls. The average is under 10% in *MEDCs*.
e.g. farming, mining, fishing and forestry.

pull factor: circumstance that attracts people to migrate.
Availability of work or better-paid work are examples of economic pull factors. The presence of hospitals and schools, or the need to live with relatives, are social pull factors.

push factor: circumstance that drives people to migrate.
Natural hazards, such as *droughts* and *earthquakes*, are physical push factors. Poverty and lack of work are economic push factors.

pyramidal peak: three-sided mountain peak with steep sides and a sharp top.
A pyramidal peak is formed by *erosion* and *weathering* on the backwalls of three or more *corries*. As the backwalls of the corries are pushed backwards, the size of the rock between them is reduced. At the same time, the rock is sharpened and made steeper.
e.g. the Matterhorn in the Alps.

quarrying: removal of rocks and minerals from the surface of the ground.

▨ Quarrying is a *primary industry*. The rocks most frequently quarried are those with economic uses, such as limestone for cement and slate for roofing. Quarrying leaves a large hole on the surface. The hole may later be used as a *landfill site.*

quaternary industry: modern, *high-tech industry* based upon research and development.

▨ The name 'quaternary' is used because this type of industry developed fourth after *primary*, *secondary* and *tertiary*. Occupations in quaternary industry are mainly found in *MEDCs*. Only a small percentage, under 5% of the working population, are employed in the quaternary sector. Knowledge gained in MEDCs through quaternary industry eventually spreads to *LEDCs*. This is an example of *invisible trade*.

▨ *e.g.* designing and assembling microelectronics for computers and tele-communications; training and advice.

rainfall: water droplets which fall onto the Earth's surface from clouds.

■ Rainfall is the main type of *precipitation*. It results from the cooling of rising air. After it reaches its *dew-point*, moisture in the air condenses into cloud (see *condensation*). Droplets of water join together in the cloud until they become too heavy to be held and fall as rain. There are three types of rainfall, classified according to the way in which the air is forced to rise:

• *frontal rainfall* — warm air rises along the fronts in a depression

• *relief rainfall* — air is forced to rise over mountains

• *convectional rainfall* — heating of the ground warms the air above, which rises in convection currents

rain shadow: sheltered side of an upland area with low *precipitation*.

■ The rain shadow is located on the *leeward* side of high ground. The air is descending, which means it is warming up and less likely to produce rain.

■ *e.g.* The eastern side of the UK is drier because it is in the rain shadow of the uplands. Manchester has 860 mm of precipitation per year, but Wakefield — lying 70 km away on the eastern side of the Pennines — has 670 mm per year.

range of goods and services: maximum distance a person is prepared to travel to purchase a particular good or service.

■ People travel further to purchase *high-order* goods and services, such as furniture or visiting a theatre, which are only purchased from time to time. People are prepared to travel only short distances to purchase *low-order* goods, such as newspapers and magazines, because these are low value and purchased regularly. Each type of good and service has its own range. In general, a person buying a car or caravan (*comparison goods*) will travel further than one buying food and drink (*convenience goods*).

rapids: small *waterfalls* creating rough water flow, mainly found in the upper course of a river.

■ Rapids form where hard bands of rock outcrop in the river channel.

raw material: *natural resource* which is used as an *input* in *manufacturing industry*.

■ Raw materials include minerals and timber, as well as farm produce. They make up a higher percentage of production costs in *heavy industry* than in *light industry*. A heavy industry is therefore more likely to be located close to supplies of its raw materials.

reclamation: the process of changing land that cannot be used in its present state into useful land for farming and settlement.
■ Land typically used for reclamation includes marsh, desert and derelict areas such as pit heaps. Marsh is reclaimed by drainage, desert by *irrigation* and pit heaps by levelling and planting vegetation.
■ *e.g.* In the Netherlands, a polder is land reclaimed from the sea.

refugee: person forced to flee from their country of residence.
■ War, political unrest and disasters, such as drought and famine, all cause people to flee. The number of refugees in the world is increasing.
■ *e.g.* In recent years, there have been large numbers of refugees from Afghanistan, the Middle East and the Balkans due to political unrest and wars.

relief: height and shape of the Earth's surface.
■ Relief is a *physical factor*. It is shown by contours on Ordnance Survey maps, supported by spot heights.

relief rainfall: *precipitation* caused by the cooling of moist air after it has been forced to rise over mountains.
■ Relief rainfall increases the amount of precipitation that falls in mountainous areas, such as the Highlands of Scotland, the Lake District and Snowdonia.

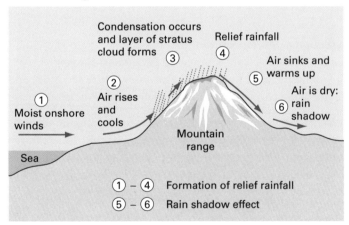

renewable resource: *natural resource* that will never run out.
■ Some natural resources, like sun, wind and water, are limitless. There is a great need to increase the percentage of energy production that comes from renewable resources. At present, *hydroelectric, wind, solar, geothermal* and *tidal power* contribute only a tiny percentage to world energy supplies. They are

mainly used for generating electricity, which is a secondary source of energy. The UK government is committed to increasing the percentage of electricity generation contributed by renewables. Energy from renewable resources is known as *alternative energy*.

Renewable energy	Percentage of UK energy production in 2000	Projected percentage in 2010
Hydroelectricity	1.4	1.4
Landfill/waste	0.6	0.8
Wind power	0.3	5.0
Solar power	0.001	0.5
Tidal power	0.0	1.0
Total	2.3	8.7

reservoir: artificial lake used to store water for human use.
- A reservoir is usually created by collecting water behind a dam built across a valley floor. Reservoirs may be used for one or more of the following:
- water supply for homes and factories
- *irrigation*
- *hydroelectric power*
- leisure activities
- *e.g.* Lake Nasser behind Aswan High Dam (Egypt).

retailing: selling goods to people from shops, stores and supermarkets.
- The newest type of retailing is e-tailing, which is selling goods over the internet.

retail park: shopping development located outside the main shopping area of the *central business district*, sometimes in an *out-of-town location*.
- Retail park shop units tend to be large. The shops, such as Comet and B&Q, often share one large car park. They are usually located next to a main road.

ribbon development: growth of a settlement in a line along the sides of a road.
- Ribbon development extends the built-up area. It leads to *urban sprawl* as separate settlements are joined together. Planners try to stop this from happening.

ribbon lake: long, thin lake on a valley floor, formed by *glaciation*.
- All ribbon lakes are formed by glacial *erosion*. As a glacier flows down a valley, areas of soft rock are eroded more than areas of hard rock. Where the rock is soft, rock basin hollows are eroded by *abrasion* and *plucking*. After the ice melts, these are filled by water to form ribbon lakes. Some are also formed by glacial *deposition*. When a glacier melts, it may deposit a *terminal moraine* which dams back water on the valley floor behind it.
- *e.g.* Windermere and Ullswater in the Lake District.

Richter scale: system used to measure the strength of an *earthquake*.

■ The higher the value on the Richter scale, the more powerful the earthquake. Earthquake shocks above 6.0 on the scale are the ones most likely to damage property and kill people. The Richter scale is a logarithmic scale. This means that when an earthquake shock measuring 5.0 is compared with stronger ones:

● a shock measuring 6.0 is 10 times more powerful
● a shock measuring 7.0 is 100 times more powerful
● a shock measuring 8.0 is 1,000 times more powerful

rift valley: steep-sided and straight valley formed between two roughly parallel *faults*.

■ Rift valleys form along *constructive plate boundaries*. Faults form as the plates are pulled apart. Land sinks in the centre between the faults.

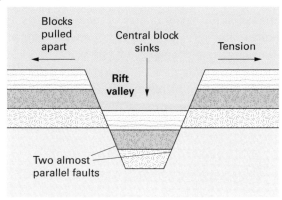

■ *e.g.* The Great East African Rift Valley.

river cliff: steep bank on the outside of a *meander*.

■ A river cliff is a landform of river *erosion*. The force of the river's flow is concentrated on the outside bend. This erodes and undercuts the river bank.

ro-ro (roll-on/roll-off): drive-on and drive-off ferry.

■ Ro-ros save time. They are used on short sea crossings.
■ *e.g.* ferries crossing the Channel from Dover to Calais and Boulogne.

rough grazing: low quality grassland.

■ In the UK, most rough grazing land is located in upland areas of moorland, such as the Lake District, and is mainly grazed by sheep. As it is of poor quality, a large area is needed to feed the animals. This is why the farming associated with rough grazing is described as *extensive farming*.

runoff: movement of water over the ground surface after *precipitation*.

■ Runoff is one of the processes in the *hydrological cycle*. Water flows over the surface until it reaches a river channel. Some factors which favour high rates of runoff include:

● very heavy rainfall (e.g. a thunderstorm)

- *impermeable rock*
- low temperature (so that there is little evaporation)

rural settlement: location with a small population, surrounded by countryside.
■ The *hierarchy* of rural settlements is: isolated farm, *hamlet, village* and very small *market town.* Anything larger than these is classified as urban rather than rural.

rural–urban fringe: area of countryside lying on the edge of a built-up area.
■ In *MEDCs,* the rural–urban fringe has mainly rural land uses, such as farms and woodland. However, some land is used for golf courses and reservoirs for water supply, which exist mainly to benefit people living in nearby towns. Some rural businesses, such as garden centres, market gardens and activities like horse riding, have grown to take advantage of the urban market. New urban developments in this zone include houses and *out-of-town* super-markets. The rural–urban fringe is an area of many conflicts. It often lies in the *green belt.* Builders and developers put great pressure on planners to allow new growth. However, many people do not want to see more of the countryside being lost.

In *LEDCs* there are some out-of-town developments in this zone, such as shopping centres, factories and new roads. However, the largest areas of land in the rural–urban fringe are often used for *shanty towns.*

saltation: bouncing of stones and boulders along the bed of a river.
- Saltation is one method by which a river transports its *load*.

savanna: area of mixed grassland and trees in the tropics.
- Savannas are tropical grasslands. Grasses are tall in the wet season, then turn brown and die away in the dry season. Trees like acacia and thorn bushes are scattered around amongst the grasses.
- *e.g.* The largest areas of savanna are in Africa where big game animals live, such as lions, giraffe and zebra. The local tribespeople are mainly pastoral nomads keeping mixed herds of cattle, goats and other animals.

science park: area laid out for *high-tech industries* connected with a university.
- Science parks are mainly research establishments, with workers in *quaternary industry*. They are attractively laid out in pleasant locations.
- *e.g.* One of the largest and most successful science parks is in Cambridge.

scree: pieces of rock with sharp edges, lying towards the foot of a slope.
- Scree is broken off the rock above by the process of *freeze–thaw*.

secondary industry: *manufacturing industry* which processes *raw materials* into finished products.
- The name 'secondary' is used because this type of industry developed after *primary industry*. Secondary industry normally happens in a *factory*. *Raw materials* need to be obtained before processing can take place. In *MEDCs* on average 30% of the working population is employed in this sector, compared with about 15% in *LEDCs*.

second home: residence where the owner spends less than half of the year.
- A second home tends to be a holiday home or weekend cottage away from the main home in the city. Some are in villages in *National Parks*, such as the Lake District, where they can be a source of conflict between owners and local residents (see diagram overleaf).

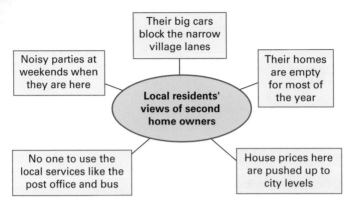

sedimentary rock: rock formed from sediments laid down on the sea bed.

■ Sedimentary rocks are arranged in horizontal layers separated by *bedding planes*. They are formed from sediments, mainly transported by rivers into the sea. These accumulate on the sea bed over a long period of time. They are upfolded by earth movements into mountains. The Alpine *fold mountains* are mainly built of limestone.

■ *e.g. chalk, Carboniferous limestone*, sandstone and clay.

seismograph: instrument which measures the strength of an *earthquake*.

service industry: see *tertiary industry*.

set-aside: *European Union* policy which pays farmers for taking land out of cultivation.

■ Set-aside is part of the *Common Agricultural Policy* to reduce over-production. Land is left to lie fallow, i.e. no crops are grown on the land, and the farmer is given compensation by the EU.

shanty town: area of poorly built, low-cost houses on land which does not have the full range of essential services.

■ Shanty towns are found in and around big cities in most *LEDCs*. Houses are made from any free or cheap materials that the residents can find, such as cardboard, wood and tin sheets. They are built on unused land and may have no water, sanitation or electricity. Most grow around the edges of cities, but some are built inside the cities on steep or swampy land which is unsuitable for building proper houses. There are many problems, such as disease and poverty. They tend to be given local names. In Brazil, they are called 'favelas'. Many shanty homes are built by migrants recently arrived from the countryside (rural–urban *migration*). When they find work, these people are keen to improve their houses, buying breeze blocks and bricks to convert the shanties into more permanent dwellings. Some organise themselves into self-help schemes for improvement. The attitude of the city authorities is important in this process. In some cities, the land is given a legal title and public services are provided. Then the shanty dwellers have more incentive to improve their homes and with time the shanty town is changed into a proper housing area. By contrast, in other cities the authorities frequently send bulldozers without warning to clear the area. The people have no chance to build anything better than the poorest of shanty homes.

shield volcano: volcanic cone with a wide base and gentle sides.

A shield *volcano* is built up by *basic lava*, which is runny and flows long distances before cooling. Most are found along *constructive plate boundaries*. Eruptions are usually non-violent, despite the great heat of the flowing lava.

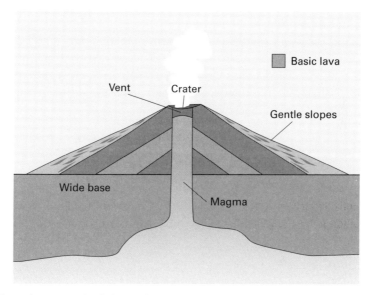

e.g. the volcanoes which form the Hawaiian islands, including Mauna Loa on Hawaii. Having grown up from the floor of the Pacific Ocean, these are some of the world's largest cones.

shifting cultivation: type of *subsistence farming* in which farmers frequently move to a new patch of land in order to grow crops.

Shifting cultivation is practised in *tropical rainforests*. For example, Indian tribes in the Amazon:

- clear a small patch of forest by slash and burn
- grow crops, such as maize and cassava, in the clearing for 2 or 3 years
- move on and clear another patch of forest

The advantage of shifting cultivation is that with small numbers of people, little permanent damage is done to the rainforest. This means that it is a *sustainable* activity. The disadvantage is that only a few people can be fed. It is not a modern method of farming.

silt: fine-grained sediment carried and deposited by rivers.

site: actual land upon which a settlement is built.
■ Favourable site factors include flat land, freedom from flooding, a south-facing position and water supply.

situation: position of a settlement in relation to the surrounding area.
■ Favourable situation factors include proximity to a junction of routes, a *bridging point* over a river or a junction between different types of area.

slip-off slope: gentle slope on the inside of a *meander*.
■ A slip-off slope is a landform of river *deposition*. Sediment is deposited where the flow of water is slow.

slum: low-quality housing in a poor residential area.
■ In *LEDCs* this is a *shanty town*. In *MEDCs* slum areas are found in the *inner city*. There are major problems:
● housing — overcrowded and lacking modern facilities, such as sanitation
● economic — high rates of unemployment and poverty
● social — crime, drugs and racism

smog: combination of smoke and fog giving poor air quality.
■ Car exhaust *pollution* leads to the formation of photochemical smog in sunny, hot weather. This causes asthma and other breathing problems.
■ *e.g.* Smog is a great problem in some cities, such as Athens and Los Angeles.

soil conservation: prevention of *soil erosion* with the aim of retaining the fertile topsoil.
■ Methods of soil conservation include:
● planting lines of trees as windbreaks
● contour ploughing going around the slope (instead of up and down)
● building terraces for cultivation on steep slopes
● planting trees on steep slopes

soil erosion: loss of the fertile topsoil by wind and water.
■ Soil erosion is most likely to occur on steep slopes in areas where rainfall is heavy. Some human activities can speed up the rate of soil erosion, such as:
● clearing trees
● ploughing straight up and down hillsides
● *overgrazing* animals
● growing just one crop on the land (*monoculture*)

solar: describes the sun as a source of light and heat.
■ Solar heating of the Earth's surface is greatest in the tropics where rates of *insolation* are highest. Recent technology, such as photovoltaic cells, is allowing solar energy to be used to make electricity. The sun is a *renewable resource* and solar power is a form of *alternative energy*. The advantages are that it is non-polluting and readily available in many parts of the world. The disadvantage

is that it is still one of the most expensive ways to generate electricity. Prices are expected to come down as technology improves.

solution: dissolving of certain minerals in water.

▨ Solution is a process of *chemical weathering. Chalk* and limestone dissolve in water and are transported in rivers in solution. *Carboniferous limestone* dissolves in rainwater made acidic by the presence of carbon dioxide in the atmosphere. The formula for limestone solution is:

$$CaCO_3 + H_2O + CO_2 \longrightarrow Ca(HCO_3)_2$$

Solution contributes to the formation of many of the features of *karst* scenery found in areas of Carboniferous limestone.

sphere of influence: area served by a settlement.

▨ The larger a settlement and the greater the number and variety of its services, the wider is its sphere of influence.

▨ *e.g.* The sphere of influence of London is the whole of the UK. Regional centres serve quite large local areas, e.g. Plymouth serves all of Devon and Cornwall. Many *market towns* serve areas of only up to 15–20 km radius.

spit: ridge of sand or shingle attached to the land at one end and finishing in the open sea at the other.

▨ A spit is a landform of coastal *deposition* formed by *longshore drift.*

▨ *e.g.* Many of the spits down the east coast of England run parallel to the coast for some distance, such as Orford Ness in Suffolk.

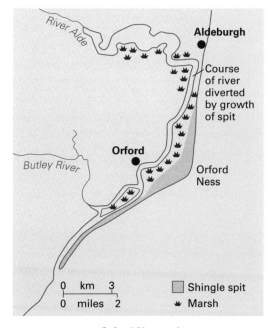

Orford Ness spit

Many of the spits along the south coast are hooked spits, which run away from the coast and end with a curve (hook) in open water. An example is Hurst Castle spit in Hampshire.

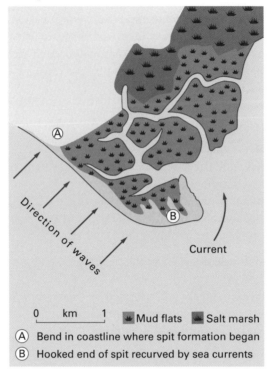

0   km   1   Mud flats   Salt marsh

Ⓐ Bend in coastline where spit formation began
Ⓑ Hooked end of spit recurved by sea currents

Hurst Castle spit

spring line: series of points where water reaches the surface from underground.
- Spring lines occur along the foot of chalk *escarpments* in southern England, where chalk meets *impermeable* clay. Water stored in the chalk emerges at the surface. A spring line is often used as the *site* of a settlement, as there is a clean and reliable supply of water.

squatter: person who sets up home on land not owned by them.
- Squatters have no legal rights to the land they are occupying. The squatter settlement which results is often the first area of housing for newcomers into cities in *LEDCs*.

stack: pillar of rock surrounded by sea and separated from the coastline.
- A stack is a landform of coastal *erosion* formed by long-continued wave action. Stacks form off coastlines of *headlands* and *cliffs* when a *cave* is opened out into an *arch*. The base of the arch is further attacked by *destructive waves*. This puts more and more pressure on the top of the arch, until it collapses, leaving the stack as an isolated slab of rock. The stack continues to be eroded and becomes a stump before being removed altogether by wave erosion.

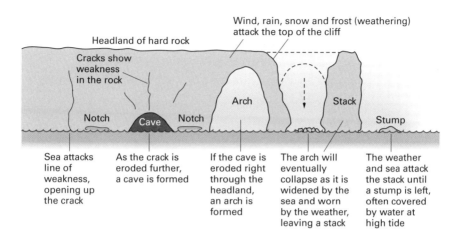

Wind, rain, snow and frost (weathering) attack the top of the cliff

Headland of hard rock

Cracks show weakness in the rock

Arch | Stack

Notch | Cave | Notch | Stump

| Sea attacks line of weakness, opening up the crack | As the crack is eroded further, a cave is formed | If the cave is eroded right through the headland, an arch is formed | The arch will eventually collapse as it is widened by the sea and worn by the weather, leaving a stack | The weather and sea attack the stack until a stump is left, often covered by water at high tide |

▨ *e.g.* the Needles off the Isle of Wight.

stalactite and stalagmite: column of lime (calcium carbonate) found in underground *caverns* and *caves* in areas of *Carboniferous limestone.*

▨ Stalactites and stalagmites are features of *karst* scenery. Stalactites hang from the ceiling. Stalagmites grow up from the ground. Lime is deposited underground when water evaporates or loses its carbon dioxide. Lime builds up very slowly, over a long period of time, from water dripping from the roofs of caves and caverns. A stalactite and stalagmite can join to form a pillar of limestone.

subduction zone: area where a rock *plate* is sinking, melting and being destroyed at a *destructive plate boundary.*

▨ The melting of the plate produces *magma* which rises and reaches the surface in places to form *volcanoes.*

subsistence farming: type of agriculture based on growing crops and rearing livestock mainly to feed the family.

▨ Subsistence farming may not produce any surplus for sale. This is the opposite of *commercial farming.* It is practised most in *LEDCs.*

▨ *e.g. Intensive farming* of rice in the Ganges valley in India. *Shifting cultivation* in the Amazon forests of Brazil. *Pastoral nomadism* in the savanna lands of Kenya.

suburb: built-up area of a town or city between the *inner city* and the edge.

▨ A suburb is that part of an urban area which has grown outwards from the old centre. At first, the spread is mainly along the sides of main roads (*ribbon development*). Then the areas in between are filled by houses. Suburbs are mainly residential, and in many urban areas of the UK they are dominated by semi-detached and detached houses built on estates. There is more space in the suburbs for larger houses, gardens and garages than in the inner city. As the suburbs continue to grow outwards, the built-up area extends into the *rural–urban fringe*. Some shopping centres, offices and factories also move to the edge of town, preferring to be nearer to their customers and workers.

sunrise industry: new growth industry, such as a *high-tech industry*.
■ Industries in decline, like many *heavy industries*, are called sunset industries.

suspension: movement of fine materials, such as sand and silt, by flowing water.
■ Suspension is one method by which a river transports its *load*.

sustainable: describes activities and economic growth which have a long future because people are working with the environment upon which they depend.
■ Sustainable *development* considers the needs of future generations as well as those of people today. The aim of sustainable development is to hand over the Earth and its resources to the next generation in the same condition that they are today. This cannot be fully achieved, but it can be helped by *conservation* and better *management* of the Earth's resources. For example, people could use more *alternative energy*.

swallow hole: funnel-shaped shaft down which a surface stream disappears underground.
■ A swallow hole is a feature of *karst* scenery which occurs in areas of *Carboniferous limestone*. Below the swallow hole is a system of underground *caverns* and *caves*.
■ *e.g.* Gaping Gill in the Yorkshire Dales.

swash: movement of water up a beach following a breaking *wave*.
■ Sand and shingle are carried up the beach with the water. Where the swash is strong, as in *constructive waves*, coastal *deposition* occurs. Where the swash is weak, as in *destructive waves*, coastal *erosion* is more likely.

tarn lake: a small round lake which fills a *corrie* hollow after the *glacier* melts.

tectonic activity: movement of the large rock *plates* of the Earth's crust.
■ The energy to move the plates comes from the Earth's internal store of heat. Tectonic activity leads to:
● *earthquakes*
● folding and the formation of *fold mountains*
● faulting and the formation of *rift valleys*
● volcanic eruptions and the formation of *composite, acid lava* and *shield volcanoes*

temperate latitudes: areas between 30° and 60° north and south of the *equator*.
■ In temperate latitudes, climates tend to be more moderate than in the areas to their north and south. Extremes of weather are unusual.

terminal moraine: ridge of material deposited at the furthest point reached by a *glacier*.
■ A terminal moraine is made of *boulder clay*. It forms when a glacier melts and dumps its entire load at the position of its front end. A terminal moraine is often larger and easier to see than other types of *moraine*. The ridge runs across the floor of the glaciated valley. In places, the mound of boulder clay acts as a dam and holds back a *ribbon lake*.
■ *e.g.* Terminal moraines are found in front of Windermere and Thirlmere in the Lake District.

tertiary industry (also called 'service industry')**:** industry that provides services to individuals and other industries.
■ Tertiary means third. These industries are called tertiary because they developed after *primary industry* and *secondary industry*. Tertiary industries provide most employment in *MEDCs* — on average 60% of the working population. In *LEDCs* the average is about 25%, but this percentage grows in size as a country increases its level of *development*.
■ *e.g.* There are many tertiary industries, including:
● public services — health, care and council services

- local services — water, gas and electricity
- transport and communications — bus, train and phone
- retail — shops, stores and supermarkets
- recreation and tourism — sports centres, hotels and cafés

threshold population: minimum number of people needed to support a good or service.

■ A lower threshold population is needed for *low-order* goods and services. The threshold population for a newsagent or a chemist is much lower than that for a clothes shop or a music store. The threshold population for a junior school is lower than that for a secondary school, which in turn is lower than that needed for a college or university. Colleges and universities are higher-order services than schools.

thunderstorm: heavy shower of rain accompanied by thunder and lightning.

■ This is *convectional rainfall*. Thunderstorms are most likely to occur in the UK in summer. Worldwide, they are most frequent in tropical areas where high rates of *insolation* heat the ground during the morning. The rain falls from tall *cumulus clouds*. These grow to great heights because of strong *convection currents* rising from the hot ground surface. Up-currents of air are even more powerful in tropical *hurricanes*, which produce some of the heaviest rainfall on Earth.

tidal power: generating electricity using the changing levels of the tide.

■ The tide is a *renewable resource* and tidal power is a form of *alternative energy*. *Barrages* are built across tidal estuaries where there is a wide range between high and low tides.

■ *e.g.* There is a tidal power barrage across the Rance estuary in France. A similar proposal for the Severn estuary in the UK has not gone ahead because of cost and possible environmental damage.

TNC: see *transnational corporation*.

tombolo: ridge of sand and shingle linking an island to the mainland.

■ A tombolo is a landform of coastal *deposition*. Tombolos are formed by *longshore drift* in a similar way to *spits* and *bars*.

■ *e.g.* Chesil Beach on the coast of Dorset.

tor: block of rock outcropping on a hill top.

■ A tor is formed by the *weathering* of rocks with many *joints*, especially granite. *Freeze–thaw* weathering widens the joints and breaks off blocks of rock.

■ *e.g.* In the UK, there are many tors on Dartmoor, an area of granite.

traction: movement of boulders by rolling along a river bed.

■ Traction is one method by which a river transports its *load*.

trade: exchange of goods and services.

■ Trade with other countries leads to *imports* and *exports*. The *European Union* encourages free trade between its member countries. It has removed tariffs and border controls to encourage and simplify the movement of goods.

transition zone: area undergoing change on the border of the *central business district* and the *inner city*.
- When a central business district grows, some city centre land uses extend into the transition zone, such as hotels, offices and car parks. Some derelict areas in the inner city may also be redeveloped for offices or used for new roads, such as inner ring roads (see *urban redevelopment*).

transnational corporation (TNC): see *multinational company*.

transpiration: loss of water from plants into the atmosphere.
- Heat causes trees and other plants to give off water vapour into the air, mainly from their leaves.

tributary: smaller stream or river which flows into a larger one.
- Tributaries increase the *discharge* of the main river. Large rivers are joined by many tributaries throughout their course. A tributary must not be confused with a *distributary*.
- *e.g.* the Missouri and Ohio are tributaries of the Mississippi.

tropical rainforest: dense forest or jungle growing in hot, wet lowlands near the equator.
- This *ecosystem* contains the greatest vegetation cover on Earth. Trees grow in layers, with a continuous canopy of tall trees below the very tall emergents. Vines and creepers grow from tree to tree. Rainforests also contain the greatest *biodiversity* on Earth. The number of known varieties of trees and plants is enormous. Climatic conditions are ideal for plant growth: it is hot (27°C) and wet (about 2,000 mm of rain per year) throughout the year. Clearance of rainforests is a major issue.

e.g. The largest area of remaining rainforest is in the Amazon Basin in Brazil. Large areas are still untouched in the Congo Basin in Africa.

Below is a brief **case study** on conflict in the Amazon Basin.

Why is the rainforest being cleared?

- The government of Brazil wants the country to develop economically.
- Logging and mining companies exploit *natural resources,* such as timber, iron ore and bauxite (for aluminium).
- Giant *hydroelectric power* schemes provide the power.
- In-migrants from other parts of Brazil settle along the sides of roads.
- New roads are planned to open up new areas of rainforest for settlement.

Who opposes rainforest clearance?

- Environmentalists believe that rainforests bring many benefits that clearance will destroy for ever (see *deforestation*).
- Indian tribes practising *shifting cultivation* are pushed off the land they have settled for hundreds of years.

The result is many conflicts of interest over rainforest clearance and its use between interested groups.

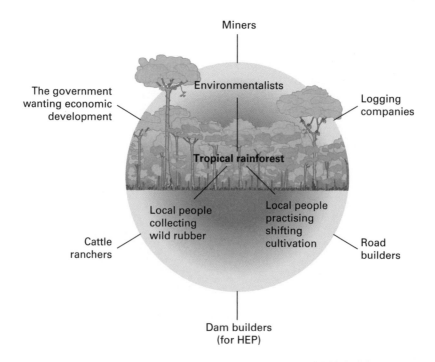

tsunami: giant sea wave travelling at high speed, often referred to as a 'tidal wave'.

■ Many tsunamis are formed after *earthquake* shocks and they are most common in the Pacific Ocean. As they reach land, they slow down and increase in size. The high wave of water smashes against the coastline, causing great destruction and loss of life.

tundra: cold, treeless land in the Arctic where the soil is permanently frozen (permafrost).

■ It is too cold for trees to grow. The natural vegetation consists of grasses, flowers, mosses and lichens.

twilight zone: run-down and derelict area of the *inner city*, associated with *urban decay*.

urban decay: decline in *inner city* areas in *MEDCs*.

■ Urban decay is associated with old, badly maintained terraced houses, and abandoned warehouses, factories and railway sidings. Better-off people move to the suburbs. These areas are also described as the *'twilight zone'* because of the many environmental, economic and social problems which develop there.

urbanisation: increase in the percentage of people living in urban areas.

■ A high percentage of people already live in towns and cities in *MEDCs*. Therefore the highest rates of urbanisation are found in *LEDCs*. This is due to:

● rural–urban *migration*

● high rates of *natural increase* of population

The graph below shows past and projected urban population data. Note that from 1950 to 1970 there was a larger urban population in MEDCs. From 1980 the figure was greatest in LEDCs.

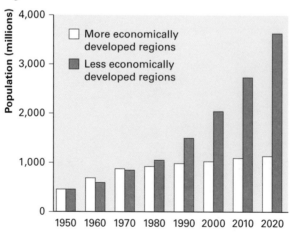

urban redevelopment: improvements in towns and cities.

■ There is most need for urban redevelopment in old, *inner city* areas. Existing buildings may be demolished and replaced by new ones. Old buildings, such as warehouses and factories, may be renovated and converted for new uses.

■ *e.g.* In the London Docklands, warehouses around old, disused dock basins have been converted into luxurious flats and apartments. In Halifax, large factory and mill buildings have been subdivided into offices. The Meadowhall out-of-town shopping centre in Sheffield is on the site of a former steel works. In Manchester, the G-MEX Exhibition Centre used to be the central railway station.

urban sprawl: outward spread of urban land uses into rural areas.

■ Urban sprawl often begins as *ribbon development* along main roads. Separate villages are surrounded and become part of the urban area. The next zone of countryside becomes the new *rural–urban fringe*. This means that the position of the rural–urban fringe is constantly changing.

U-shaped valley: glacial trough with a flat floor and steep sides.

■ The cross-profile of a U-shaped valley resembles the shape of the letter U. The valley is usually straight and deep, lined by rock outcrops and hanging-valley waterfalls. *Ribbon lakes* sometimes fill part or all of the floor. A U-shaped valley is formed by processes of glacial *erosion,* such as *abrasion* and *plucking*. A pre-existing river valley is widened and deepened as a glacier flows along it.

■ *e.g.* Many of the valleys in the Lake District and Snowdonia are of this type.

vent: vertical pipe within a *volcano* through which *magma* flows to the surface.

village: *rural settlement,* larger than a *hamlet* but smaller than a *market town.*
■ The main function of a village is residential, i.e. it is a place for people to live. It has a limited number of *low-order* services, such as a church, public house, post office and general shop. The number of these services is being reduced as more people own and use cars. Some small villages now have none of their own services.

visible trade: international *trade* in raw materials, foodstuffs and manufactured goods.
■ This is trade in goods which can be either weighed or counted.

volcano: cone-shaped mountain formed by surface eruptions of *magma* from inside the Earth.
■ Volcanoes form along *constructive plate boundaries* and *destructive plate boundaries.* The shape of the cone varies according to the type of magma erupted:
● *acid lava volcano* — cone is dome shaped with steep sides and a narrow base, formed by *acid lava*
● *shield volcano* — cone has gentle sides and a wide base, formed by *basic lava*
● *composite volcano* — a cone built of alternate layers of lava and ash, which is tall with a perfect cone shape

V-shaped valley: river valley with steep and high slopes.
■ The cross-profile of a V-shaped valley resembles the shape of the letter V. The centre of the valley is deepened more than the rest by processes of river *erosion,* such as *abrasion* and *hydraulic action.* Valleys are deeper and steeper in the upper course of a river. Rivers cut down most in this section because they are flowing high above sea level.

warehouse: building for the temporary storage of goods.
■ Goods are distributed from warehouses to retailers and users. In the past, most warehouses were located next to rivers for easy distribution. Many of these buildings are no longer used. Some have been pulled down or converted into other uses, such as offices and apartments. Most modern warehouses are built next to motorways for easy distribution. For example, supermarket companies such as Tesco and Asda have warehouses from which their lorries supply the shops.

warm front: dividing line between warm and cold air, where the warm air is being forced to rise.
■ Ahead of a warm front, rising warm air cools and this leads to the formation of a band of cloud and rain. After a warm front passes over a place, cold air is replaced by the *warm sector* of a *depression*.

warm sector: warm air at the surface in the centre of a *depression* between the *warm* and *cold fronts*.
■ Within the warm sector, the weather is usually warmer, less cloudy and drier than along the fronts.

water cycle: see *hydrological cycle*.

waterfall: landform where water in a river drops vertically.
■ Waterfalls form along rivers where a hard band of rock outcrops. Softer rocks below the hard band are more easily eroded to leave a vertical drop over which the water falls. The force of the falling water forms a *plunge pool*. Over time, the waterfall retreats upstream, leaving a *gorge*. In glaciated valleys, tributary streams are left hanging at a higher level than the more heavily eroded main valley floor. These streams cascade down into the main valley as *hanging valley* waterfalls.

watershed: ridge of higher land between the *drainage basins* of two rivers.
■ A watershed separates the directions in which rivers flow.

water table: level where the ground is saturated (the soil and rock cannot hold any more water).
- The level of the water table is usually below the surface. It rises and falls according to amounts of *precipitation* and rates of *evapotranspiration*. In the UK it is usually higher in winter when more rain falls and less water is evaporated. The water table reaches the surface where springs occur, as along the *spring line* at the foot of a *chalk escarpment*.

water vapour: water held in the form of a gas in the atmosphere.
- Water in its liquid form is heated to become water vapour. Water vapour returns to the liquid form as a result of cooling and *condensation*.

wave: long body of sea water which breaks forwards as it reaches the coastline.
- A wave releases energy as it breaks. This leads to coastal *erosion* and *deposition*, depending upon the type of wave. *Destructive waves* erode, while *constructive waves* deposit.

wave-cut platform: gently sloping surface of rock exposed at low tide.
- A wave-cut platform is a landform of coastal *erosion*, formed at the bottom of *cliffs*. It is left behind as cliffs are eroded and forced to retreat inland by processes of erosion such as *abrasion* and *hydraulic action*.

weather: condition of the atmosphere at any given time.
- Weather describes day-to-day variations in temperature, *precipitation*, cloud and wind. The UK's weather is characterised by frequent change and great variability. When weather conditions are averaged over a period of about 30 years, this gives the *climate* of a place.

weathering: breakdown of rock in the place where it outcrops.
- Weathering occurs where rock is open to attack from the weather. Some rocks are full of weaknesses, such as *joints*, which speed up the rate at which weathering occurs. There are three main types of weathering:
- *physical weathering*, e.g. *freeze–thaw*
- *chemical weathering*, e.g. *solution* of *Carboniferous limestone*
- *biological weathering*, e.g. tree roots breaking up rock

westerlies: *prevailing winds* over the British Isles.
- Blowing from the west and associated with *depressions*, westerlies bring wet and windy weather to the UK. The western side of the UK is wetter and windier than the east. The east is on the *leeward* side of the uplands in the *rain shadow*.

wind break: line of trees providing shelter against strong, cold or *prevailing winds*.
- Wind breaks are planted to:
- provide shelter for crops

- stop soil erosion
- make living conditions more comfortable in isolated settlements

wind power: generating electricity using the force of the wind.

■ Wind is a *renewable resource* and wind power is a form of *alternative energy*. Advanced technology has improved the design of wind turbines, reducing the cost of producing electricity in this way. Several wind turbines are usually placed together in areas where physical conditions encourage high wind speeds, such as on hill tops or along the coast. This is called a wind farm. The main problem with wind power is that it is not always windy. The existence of wind farms does not mean that other power stations can be closed down, because they are still needed on non-windy days. Some people also object to the noise and appearance of wind farms.

■ *e.g.* Wind farms are found both onshore and offshore at Blyth in Northumberland.

zero population growth: when the *birth rate* equals the *death rate*.

■ With zero population growth the rate of *natural increase* is 0.

■ *e.g.* In Spain in 1999 both birth and death rates were 9.4 per 1,000. However, Spain's population did increase by 0.9 per 1,000 because of *immigration*.